Doctor in the House

DOCTOR IN THE HOUSE

ALEX RUDD

LUME BOOKS

LUME BOOKS

This edition published in 2021 by Lume Books
30 Great Guildford Street,
Borough, SE1 0HS

ISBN 978-1-83901-323-2

Typeset using Atomik ePublisher from Easypress Technologies

www.lumebooks.co.uk

Author's Note

First of all I just want to repeat what I think I said after I wrote my first book, *London Call-Out: Confessions of a Doctor in the Capital*, about my more exciting time dashing across London in the small hours as a night-time, out-of-hours doctor. I wanted to say then that I'm a trained doctor, not a trained writer. So do please forgive me for all the mistakes I may have made when I type all this up. To my fellow doctors, I've actually tried to write for ordinary people, my non-medical friends, so apologies if you think it's not all 'textbook quality'. I've tried to be as honest as I can to my memories and my notes of all the incidents I've attended. But I've also tried really hard to change lots of details to protect the privacy and dignity of the people and places I have seen. So if a few things get mixed up in that mix then I really do apologise. Sorry, as well, if you think I digress a bit sometimes and go on about a few of the challenges of the doctor's job. I'm not always totally politically correct. But I genuinely try to just raise the questions that deserve to be asked. And of course sorry if you think I've focused too much on a few unusual cases, or too much on a few dull ones. I tried to get the mix right here, though I know I could have failed. With all that said, why did I write the books in the first place? I suppose one reason is that I love reading about the different jobs other people do. I read the memoirs of fire-fighters, police-officers, soldiers and all sorts of others. I love getting a window into other working worlds. So when Endeavour Press said I could open a window into the world of a freelance GP I thought I'd give it a try.

I do hugely enjoy my job. If you're a people person then this is a great career, because you do meet a constant stream of new faces. You see people at their best and at their worst. Every doctor will say the system can make things so much tougher than it needs to be. Every doctor will talk about ever changing new challenges. But I hope this book shows that we really do thrive on the pressure and strive to do the best we can for all our patients.

Alex Rudd, London, 2015.

Chapter One: New Starts.

I don't want to be a vampire any more. I've worked nights for nearly three years now. I've been one of London's secret doctors, a full-time, night-time GP doing the house calls no-one else wants to do. I've seen a lot of drama and sadness in the small hours of the morning. But now it's time to see a bit of sunshine. I'm going to work the day shift for a change.

I'm still going to be a locum, though. I'll still turn up at different, random surgeries every day. I'll fill in when their existing doctors are off sick, on holiday, on a course, having a baby or are just too ground-down by the whole crazy system to show up for work. I'll still be happy to do my share of house calls in the afternoons and at the weekend. But I'll no longer have to get into a freezing cold car to race around the capital to do those calls at 3am. Instead I'm going to sit in an endless series of nice, warm surgeries in the daylight. I'm going to deal with an endless series of nice, pleasant people and I'm going to enjoy the easy life for a while. Because that's what it's like being a London locum in the day, right?

Oh dear. What, exactly, was I thinking?

I start to learn the truth on my very first day-time shift. Or just before it, to be exact. I'm nice and early but there's no-one there to let me into the surgery. I'm in what I thought was a posh, polite part of town. We're a little bit south of the river, near a whole load of those old warehouses that are now zillion pound apartments.

The outside of the surgery door is covered with notices. There seem to be an awful lot of things the patients are not allowed to do inside. No smoking, of course. And no eating or drinking. No mobile phone use either. Good luck with that one, I think, as I peruse the rest of the list. No threatening or abusive language or behaviour. Quite right too. No to racism and bullying either, which surely ought to go without saying. No bikes or scooters, oddly enough. No chance of seeing a doctor if you're late, another note says, taking a different tack. No entry once the surgery has closed. And then, right at the end and sort of back to the bikes and the scooters, we're told there's no skateboarding either. Quite a while has passed while I've read all that. It's a bit of a downer, if I'm honest. So I'm a little bit punch drunk from all the negativity as I ring the well-hidden doorbell half an hour before my surgery is due to start. I wait to be buzzed through the locked entry door. No-one replies. I'm not buzzed through and it's cold outside. I ring the bell again. Nothing. I pull the booking sheet out of my bag to see if there's a contact number to call. There is and when I try it I can just about hear a phone ringing somewhere through the double doors. No-one answers it. But I can see some movement inside the building. A light goes on and something seems to be happening. So hopefully my first day-time shift won't be over before it's even begun.

The pinched, pale face of an older lady appears, suddenly, in the small panel of reinforced glass on the surgery door. I only just stop myself from stepping backwards in surprise, if not shock. How did she get there so fast and so quietly? Did she tip-toe? Is she trying to scare me?

'I'm your doctor,' I mouth through the glass. I hold up my booking sheet with my agency details on the top.

The woman doesn't even shrug. I'm not sure if she looks blank, disinterested or both. Both, I decide, in the end. 'I'm your locum doctor!' I repeat, a little louder. 'I'm your extra GP for today.'

The woman moves back from the glass, to look me up and down. She looks annoyed. I'm holding up my NHS lanyard and ID now. These people have asked for an extra GP today. Surely they are expecting one?

My sinister gate-keeper sighs deeply as she considers the situation at great length. Then she slowly and unwillingly reaches out and unlocks the door.

'Good morning. I'm Doctor Alex Rudd. I'm your GP for the day,' I begin as cheerily as I can, deciding to put the bad start behind us and offer the hand of friendship.

'Uh huh,' she says ignoring my hand entirely. I've stepped inside by now and she locks the door behind me. I pull back my hand, feeling a bit socially inept. Then the gate-keeper heads back towards the reception area. 'Then I'll come right this way,' I mutter under my breath as I follow her. At which point I do actually speak out loud. The lady is heading through a 'Staff Only door' towards the reception area. 'You are expecting me, I hope,' I say. 'Where would you like me to go?'

'Room Three,' she says, without even turning round. That's

two words. Apart from 'Uh-huh' that's the only thing she's said so far.

I can't actually be bothered to deal with her any more so I head down a short corridor to where I assume Room Three to be. The door is locked. So I will have to speak to my new best friend again.

'The room door is locked,' I say, opening the Staff Only door and daring to go inside. I'm half expecting my new friend to scream at me for invading her kingdom. She doesn't. She's sitting at a desk with a mug of tea in front of her. She's not on the phone, she's not doing any work and she's not reading a newspaper, a book or a magazine. She's just there. Motionless, calm and entirely blank. 'The room door is locked,' I repeat. Is the woman actually unwell? There's the longest and most unnecessary sigh in the world before she rises and shrugs. She opens a cabinet behind her and produces a set of keys. 'I need them back,' she says, without a flicker of emotion.

Again I can't be bothered to engage. I head back towards the corridor and two other women with keys are coming through the outside door. 'Hello. I'm Alex Rudd. I'm your locum doctor for the day,' I say.

They both say 'Hello' in passing and continue towards the Staff door. That's one word from each of them. I've still had less than a dozen words in total since I arrived. I do at least get just the hint of a smile from these newcomers. But it's not exactly a welcome. No wonder the full-time GP has gone off sick. I'd say that working here must be like working in a morgue or a funeral home. But like most doctors I've spent a fair bit of time in both places over the years. Both are a lot jollier than this.

I move on. My consulting room is perfectly adequate. I take the keys back to the staff room and I do get a single words of thanks from the gate-keeper. A breakthrough, I think. And I may need one. Because I know now I have to head back to my new desk to face the horror of the surgery's computer system.

I swear that NHS computers are the worst part of the locum life. You'd think they'd all be the same. We all do the same job, for the same organisation. But computers are like patients. Infinitely variable. And often infinitely annoying. Today it looks as if I need a log on code and password, both of which I don't have, of course. I do recognise most of the programmes on the screen when I get to it after another unwelcomed visit to the reception area. But where the printer is or how it works and whether or not it has plain or prescription paper will remain a mystery for some time. I already know that in a place like this I'll never find a urine bottle when I need one. I'll run out of x-ray forms and I won't have a clue how to print out any more. And as for an auroscope? Forget it. Could be anywhere. There's a great quote from the people at the National Association of Sessional GPs – the people I couldn't function without. One of its other members famously wrote up the fact that in three months he worked in forty different rooms, in twenty different practices, using six different clinical software systems, twenty different types of printer and six different referral pathway systems. Oh, and he saw 1,300 patients.

And it's time for me to see the first of mine. By the sound of it the surgery doors are now open. My first patients are starting to arrive. For the past three years doing out-of-hours work I've learned what goes bump in the night. Now I'm going to find out what goes down in the day.

Chapter Two: The First Day.

THREE relatively uneventful patients in and I get the first tough case of the day. And it's a typically sad one. It's a charming looking lady who looks to be in her fifties. She's nicely dressed with thin greying hair that must once have been blond. She's got soft, kind eyes and a warm but worried face. She wafts in on a thick cloud of sweet-smelling talcum powder and very strong perfume. And is there, also, the hint of something else in the air?

'I've got a little bit of a problem,' she begins. She sits down, very unwillingly. Her soft brown eyes are downcast now. It's clear that she doesn't want to look at me. She doesn't want to be here. All of a sudden there's something infinitely still and very, very sad about this quiet, determined lady.

I wait for her to speak, giving a half-smile of encouragement, even though she's still looking anywhere but at me. As she settles on the chair, breathing too deeply and taking far longer than she needs to get comfortable, I can definitely smell something else through all the perfume and the talc. It's something a little bit putrid and a whole lot worrying. I give another smile she doesn't see and I give her a few more moments to settle. If she doesn't speak soon I'll have to prompt her and get this going – the surgery clock is ticking as usual. But we're not quite there yet.

'It's been going on for a little while now. It's got a little bit worse, I think. I've tried to hide it. I've tried to cover it up. But I knew I had to come in and see someone, in the end.' All of a sudden the words come out in a disconcerting, unwilling rush. There's still no eye contact. She won't look at me, but I look at her. The warm, wide eyes are very wet now. The sudden stillness and the overwhelming sadness is palpable. I like this lady, I think unaccountably. But I fear for her.

She said she has tried to cover it up. Covering it up with all the talc and the perfume, I imagine. And what is the 'it' that's overcome her? It could still be very many things. But I'm getting some clues. I'm making some deductions. And I need her to tell me more.

'And what is the problem?' I ask gently. 'Just tell me. That's what I'm here for.'

Again, very unwillingly, my patient prepares to tell me. She indicates her right breast. Then, with horrible resignation, she gets on with things. She has decided it is time to act, possibly because it's easier to do this than to speak. She moves to open the top buttons of her pale blue blouse. She pulls a tired-looking bra aside and I lean forward a tiny bit to look. As I do, I try not to gag. The smell isn't just stronger now. It's intense. It's a shocker. It's rotting flesh. The worst I've smelt in some time. And I've smelt more than my fair share as a night time out-of-hours doctor doing inner London house calls for the very sick and the very disenfranchised.

'OK, let me take a closer look.' I say calmly. My own eyes are watering now, but not, like hers, from fear or sadness.

I lean in. I'm looking at what appears to be a wide open wound on the side of the patient's right breast, just above and to the right of the nipple. It's weeping, despite all the drying talc that's been emptied all across it. What I can see looks to be alive. Protruding through the middle of it, causing it, in fact, is what I fear, and almost certainly know, is the cancerous tumour. This has been growing inside her for some time. For far, far too long. It's the lump women – and indeed men – should check for. It's the one they should get examined as soon as it's felt. The one that can be tackled, destroyed and removed by so many of the tools we have at our disposal. Or it is the one that can be ignored and can lie in wait, growing, expanding, getting tougher and, in the end, pushing right through the skin of the breast, erupting and coming out into the open. It's one of the very many shocking things that can happen in our otherwise immaculately designed bodies. It's a killer that grows inside. And in this case, it has grown so much it's run out of room. It's done something most people don't realise is possible. It's breached the barrier. It's on show now. It's awful. And this quiet, dignified and surely intelligent woman must know she should have tackled this so long ago.

'And how long did you say this has been going on for?' I ask softly as I carry on with a light examination. We both know the simple answer to the question. For far, far too long.

'For a few months now. Maybe more.'

'And how did it begin?'

She shrugs. 'With just a lump, I suppose. I know that's a cliché. It was something I felt, that felt a little odd. A lump. The kind we're supposed to watch out for. I'm not a fool.'

I give her the dignity of a nod of agreement. It's clear she's not a fool. Except, of course, about this. 'And did you see anyone about it?' I ask, already knowing her answer.

'I thought it might go away,' she says. There is the shortest of pauses. I wonder how often we GPs hear those six, sad words in our careers. I thought it might go away. It doesn't, I want to say. It never does. Instead it does this.

'So this is where you are now,' I say, stating the obvious and telling my patient she can get covered up again. There's not a lot of doubt about what's going on here. There's not a lot more I need to see or to do or to know. It's time to talk – and my patient gets ahead of me. A rush of words come out again. The floodgates are fully open now. The worst moment must have been showing me the problem. Facing the embarrassment, the awkwardness, the odour. Now she's done that she has a moment of control. She takes it.

'It seemed to get worse. It was about three weeks ago – maybe more - when it really got bad. It seemed to break through the skin. It was the most awful, terrifying thing. It was like a nightmare. I just wanted to go back, to go back in time. I wanted another chance to face up to it at the start. But I couldn't. So I ignored it again. I tried to go to work, to carry on. And every single moment I was afraid. I tried to pretend, to hope, to beg that every night, every morning, it might have gone away. That I'd be saved from it somehow. That I wouldn't be such an idiot, such a sad, sad foolish old woman.' She gulps now, sucking in air in a rush. She still can't look right at me. But she does throw me sudden, anguished glances. She's gripping the side of her chair tightly now. Her pale, thin hands are white with terrible tensions. And the rush of words starts again. 'Then it seemed to get infected, somehow. I wanted to be wrong. I wanted it to go away. I thought if I got more sleep, if I was calmer, less worried, less stressed then it would go away. But it didn't. It got worse. It got bigger. I was so scared, I just couldn't breathe.'

'You put talc on to soothe it? And for the odour?' I ask, trying to move her on.

'Mainly to try and hide the smell. Nothing really soothes it.'

I lean back a tiny bit in my chair and try to give what I want to be a reassuring and confident look. What seems eminently clear is that this lady has what's called fungating breast cancer. Fungating, which sounds like fungal, isn't actually the cause of the rotting smell. The word really just means breaking out, the breaching of the skin a bit like a mushroom breaks through the soil. It's this, the necrotic dead tissue and the infection that it's triggered, that must be making the lady retch every morning when she wakes up and tries to wash. Tries to wash with I'd imagine a huge amount of pain, embarrassment, fear and regret.

'I'm glad you're here at last, that's a good thing,' I begin.

'And the bad thing?'

'There is no bad thing,' I lie, cursing my stupid choice of words. Despite her position, this lady is as sharp as nails. 'But I'm sure you're aware we need to get this checked out properly as soon as we can. I can book you into the breast clinic right now. I can make the call myself. They're a great team of people, this is what they deal with every day and they'll be able to see you fast. This is the right thing to do. It's good we're going it now.'

This proud, primly-dressed lady's eyes are entirely moist with tears now. She's holding it all in, but it doesn't look easy for her.

'Do you have people you can talk to about this? Family or friends, not medical people?' I ask as I fish out the numbers I need.

My patient looks past me, trying to think, her eyes glistening all the more. 'I live on my own,' she says flatly. There's another long pause. Her eyes look to the distance. She's thinking. Is there anyone she can call? 'There are the girls at work,' she says, in the end. Then she sighs, seeming to be defeated. 'But they're all so young. They've all been talking about this, I know. They've smelt it. They can't bear it. I see it on their faces. It's been so, so difficult. I can't speak to any of them about it. They wouldn't understand. They're so young. They go to lunch together every day. I can't speak to them. I'll be fine.'

But will she? I feel a sudden stab of sympathy for this dignified older lady. She lives alone. And when she's trying to think of any friends she can lean on, the only ones she can come up with are the young girls she barely knows at work. The ones who go for lunch together, without her, every day. She's alone. She shouldn't be. But this is where she is. And you know what? There are things that can change here. The people at the breast clinic will listen. They are amazing. And they are just the start. There are so many places they'll be able to direct her to see, so many contacts she can make. We should be so proud, in this country, of the support we can offer when the chips are down. We beat ourselves up so often, slamming the NHS, the country, the system. And yes, on a grand, national scale there are problems. But when it comes to individuals there is help, support, charity and a deep well of human kindness. I want her to feel it.

I curse under my breath that we're in such an unfriendly, unwelcoming surgery as I carry on scratching around for the contact details I need. Then I have to find out how to get through to them on a phone system that seems to be locked. It takes me longer than it should to set everything up for this patient. And I hate that. It makes it seem as if the next step may be hard, when I want to show that it's easy. I know there are a thousand reasons why this proud, scared and lonely lady didn't ask for help sooner. Could one of them have been all the negative signs on the surgery door? Or the pinched, angry face of the lady at the reception desk? I dismiss the idea as I hand over the details of the breast clinic and a few other pieces of paper that will help her. As I do so I notice that there seem to be clocks all around the consulting room. There's a big one above the door. Another behind the desk. A third on a shelf. Whoever works here normally must be a stickler for time-keeping. And I realise that I've spent far more than the allocated ten minutes with this most fragile of women.

'You've taken the first and the hardest step by coming in. It was overdue but it's not too late. You will pursue this, won't you?' I ask. 'You must go to see these people. They are expecting you, they know the situation so you don't need to explain it all again from scratch. They will support you. They'll understand and they'll help. Whenever I deal with them I'm amazed at how kind and enthusiastic these people are. They're specialists and they can turn into friends. There's so much they can and will do for you. Don't be afraid of this. Be excited. Make sure you're there. Promise me?'

My patient nods and gives a weak smile that in the past must have lit up a room. 'I promise. I do promise,' she says. Then she sighs, clearly emotionally exhausted. 'I know I've been stupid, so very stupid,' she says. There is a long, sad expression on her face that is neither a smile nor a frown. She looks right at me, for the very first time. 'Thank you,' she says. Then she gets up and she's gone. Those two words are the ones I will value for the rest of the day. They will see me through whatever happens next in this surgery.

I tap away the computer to update the patient notes. As a locum I know all too well that I'm unlikely to see this lady again or to ever find out what happens to her. I probably won't come back to this practice and if I do it's unlikely to be the day she comes back in – if indeed she ever does. How close could she be to the end? Closer, perhaps, than even she fears. And her fears are so very real. I think of her very briefly, heading home on her own. I think of her sitting in her office full of young people she thinks won't understand her. They will understand her, I'm sure. They will ask you to join them for lunch, I want to tell her. But she's gone. It's too late to tell her that now.

Chapter Three: Tall Tales.

A teenage lad shuffles into the surgery next. He's in typical teenage kit, gravity-defying jeans, un-laced trainers and a zipped up hoody. It's as if he's a youth from central casting, but somehow he's not quite pulling it all off. Someone else could wear the exact same things and look cool. This guy doesn't do the same. As someone who was never in the cool crowd at school I understand him. I know that not everyone fits in, all the time.

'So, how can I help you?' I ask.

'I'm too short. I want to be taller,' he blurts out.

He's sitting down already and I size him up at about five foot six. If he was well below his age to height ratio I could refer him to an endocrinologist for tests and possible treatment. But it's clear he's nowhere near needing this. 'How old are you?' I ask, so I can be sure.

'Sixteen. Nearly.'

'Well you've got plenty of time to grow,' I begin, ready to knock this on the head but trying not to sound patronising. He dismisses my words as, well, patronising.

'I know all that. But I'm one of the shortest people in my school. I'm running out of time.'

'That's not true. You're not running out of time. Boys get big growth spurts till they're a lot older than you, you're only at the start' I say, regaining control of the conversation. 'People can grow steadily, sometimes slowly, for years. They fill out, as well. People bulk up as well as getting taller. And boys, as I'm sure you know, often grow slower than girls. They keep growing for longer so if you feel as if you're falling behind you can catch up. You can keep growing till you're maybe twenty-one. You've plenty of time yet.'

'I need to find a treatment.'

I sigh. 'Well there's nothing we can offer. You really are well within normal limits for your age. Do you want me to get an exact height for you?' I indicate a tatty old chart on the wall. The lad shuffles over to it. He's very, very unwilling to step out of those pimped up trainers. It's clear he jealously guards the extra centimetres they give him. But in the end he gives them up and stands in his socks. Stands and tries to stretch every vertebrae in his body.

'One hundred and sixty-five centimetres. That's five foot five – just over. That's OK, totally OK,' I say.

But it's not OK to my patient. He grabs his stacked-up trainers like a drowning man grabs a life-raft. He pulls them on fast. He's happier now. And he's got more to say. 'I have a raw egg, mixed in full fat milk, every night,' he begins defiantly.

'That's a lot of fat and protein,' I say. 'It's probably not going to help you that much, if I'm honest,' I say, about to continue before he cuts me off.

'I want to know what else I can take,' he says in a rush. 'And

16

I know there are things I can take. I just want to know which ones and where to get them.'

This next bit could be important. 'Well there are all sorts of protein drinks and shakes you can try,' I start. 'But I have to tell you that they're more for bulking up at the gym than growing your actual frame.'

'Steroids,' he interrupts. 'I need steroids.'

I look right at him. He so doesn't need steroids. 'They won't help with your frame, your height,' I start. 'And they can make everything worse for you. I can't stop you from doing anything you want to do. But promise me this. If you ever think seriously about taking steroids then go online and read the horror stories first. Google it. Search for something like: side effects of steroids. You'll read about guys who lose their hair, whose testicles shrink, who get massive acne, who can't sleep and get delusional. Your teeth can go weird, and your sperm count can go down. Do you want any of that? You can get mood swings as well. You'll read about young guys who die. We see this, as doctors. We know the damage that steroids can do. Buying it online or from some dodgy bloke at the gym is never going to end well. If you say you want them to make you taller they'll say they'll do that, because they want your money. They'll be lying.'

I can't waste too much time on this, but there's one other point I want to make. I know there's a whole sub-culture of steroid users and pushers who peddle all sorts of lies. I want to knock a few on the head. 'And really quickly you need to know you don't just get all the bad stuff if you inject. People will say the pills or the creams or the gel's aren't as bad. They are. They'll cost you huge amounts of money, they'll do you all this damage and they won't make you taller. They won't make you grow. That is going to happen naturally. You probably don't feel young, but you are. Get on with other things. Time is on your side.'

The teenager is nodding, but I've no idea if he's really listening. And as he's not strictly ill I've probably given him all the time I can. Too much time, my colleagues might say.

'The last thing is just to stay healthy. It's obvious, isn't it? If you take some bad stuff, even if you drink or smoke too much it will hit your body. You really do have several more years to grow. So give yourself the best shot.'

He shuffles out the surgery the way he had shuffled in. Had I managed to avoid being an utterly patronising old fart? Had I come over like a sad old Geography teacher? I hope yes to the first question and no to the second. And at least I'd not told him to stand up straight or that girls care more about personality than height. Anyway, I can't worry about it. I close his notes and move on. An unlikely noise is coming from the waiting area. Someone seems to be playing the guitar. And in a busy medical surgery that's never good news.

Chapter Four: An Itchy Interlude.

'How can I help you today?' I ask, watching as a very shaggy, twenty-something man manoeuvres his guitar through my surgery door. His music hadn't been too bad, if I'm honest. But the fact that he thought it was appropriate to play in our waiting area is enough to set off some warning bells.

'It's my balls,' the man begins, a faint European accent and a clear sense of pride in his voice.

'OK, what about them?' I ask, a feeling of dread in my mind. Are they enormous, or something? What could this be about?

'They itch.'

Ah. Crabs or scabies, I think.

'They've been itching for nearly a year. I've been here nearly twenty five times. Nothing ever gets done,' he says.

I glance at my screen and look at his file. He has, indeed been here time and time again about the same scratchy problem. And he has, of course, got mental health issues flagged up with some psychotic episodes, some paranoia, some voices in his head, some aggression and violence.

But when it comes to his balls, a quick read of the notes say the previous doctors have done exactly what I would have done on his first, fifth or, now, what could almost be his twenty-fifth visit. He's been examined, he's been to GUM clinics. He hasn't been found to have any nasty little creatures rummaging around down there. Among many other things he has, however, had some tubes of antibiotic cream prescribed which he says have helped him. He's wanted more, but an earlier doctor here refused to repeat the offer. Now it's my turn.

'Let's take a look,' I say, hoping he's had a shower. A quick examination doesn't suggest very much. I don't see any evidence of an infestation. Not even athlete's foot, or dhobie itch.

So what's going on? With so little to go on my gut feeling is to de-medicalise this and stop my guitar player from feeling a prescription will always be the answer to his problems. I'm also convinced there's one very good reason why his balls itch. Because he keeps scratching them.

'I want to see a dermatologist,' he says as I finish my exam and get him to pull his jeans back up.

I scroll through his record again. 'You saw a dermatologist in August. You came back with nothing out of the ordinary. Nothing that needed treatment.'

'I want to see a different dermatologist,' he counters.

I tell him I'm not seeing any reason to refer him again and start to say that a second opinion is unlikely to be any different to the first. At which point he says – at great length – that he'll make an official complaint against me. He gets all the jargon right in his wild and angry little speech. He knows his rights, this man. He knows the quangos and the patient advocate groups and all the layers of officialdom that will take his side and feed his sense of injustice and entitlement.

So how far will he take this? Another look at his file suggests that he really does have form when it comes to official complaints. I wouldn't be the first doctor, receptionist or consultant he's spoken out against. I wonder, briefly, just how much NHS time and money this man has taken up on appointments, examinations, referrals, repeats, prescriptions and complaints over the past twelve months. And the twelve months before that.

'And do not tell me that it is all in my mind. That's what the last one said,' he adds suddenly, his accent thicker and a new, darker tone in his voice.

'But do you not think that some of it could be in your mind?' I begin. 'When was the last time you spoke to anyone about things like this?'

'I'm talking to you, no? I want some more of the cream that worked last time.'

'I mean talking to someone about all sorts of things. Talking around everything. That can help. It can move your focus on. I think the more you think about your balls the more you'll worry about what's going on. Think about everything else and I bet you nothing will be going on. You do know it's possible to imagine an itch? Imagine that your foot itches, for example, and it will. Think of something else and it's gone.'

He doesn't care. 'I want the cream.'

And I'm not going to prescribe it. I feel like I'm house-training a puppy or dealing with a small child. I have to set the boundaries here. I'm not going to be the soft-touch locum who dolls out prescriptions like sweets, just because they want to clear their list and have an easy life.

'So you're not going to give me anything, no?' He challenges when I give him the news.

'Not today, no. I cannot see any medical reason why your balls are itching, and all the information says that other, fuller examinations have had the same conclusion. Try and stop scratching your balls, stop playing with them, and the problem will go away.' And then I hear myself say it. 'And if it doesn't, then come back in a couple of weeks.' I hate myself for pushing the man on to some other doctor some other time. Because it's clear he – and his guitar - will be back.

I run through all the other patients on my list. They're a blur, if I'm honest, as I try to win back a bit of time and catch up with the note-taking and the admin. And so, suddenly, the first day of my new life doing the day shift is over.

I had signed up to do a four hour stretch this morning. I was allocated nearly two dozen patients, I had at least four no-shows and I think roughly as many extras squeezed in at the end. I like to think I've helped the practice keep to its targets and to get through the day. And while I don't earn as much as some newspaper headlines suggest, I will get a nice amount of money for it. So it's a good job I'm not expecting any thanks as well.

My oh-so un-friendly friend at reception is still there when I head into her sanctum to get the key to lock up my consulting room door. The other two staff are tapping away at screens and one picks up a phone as I enter. But the first lady is doing what she was doing at the start of the day. Just sitting there, almost motionless. She's not reading, she's not writing, she's not speaking. Extraordinary.

I lock my surgery and return the key. 'Well, thanks for all your help,' I say, deciding that sarcasm could be my highest form of wit. I get a quick glance and a smile from the other ladies. Nothing from the boss. 'Well, that's me done. Goodbye,' I say, defeated.

'Uh-huh,' she says.

Chapter Five: Out of Africa.

THREE days later and I'm in a far friendlier surgery. It's been a busy morning and as my latest patient leaves the room I sneak out to run to the loo. I'm on my way back when I hear it. The receptionist at the front desk is leaning across to speak to an elderly lady.

'Doctor Kay isn't here today, I'm afraid,' she's saying in an exaggerated whisper. 'You'll be seeing Doctor Rudd. He's only a locum.'

He's only a locum.

I'm shaking my head a little as I go back to my temporary surgery, click on the call-button and wait for yet another mildly disappointed patient to walk into the room. Yes, I'm a locum – but I'm still a fully trained and experienced doctor. As a locum I fill in the gaps and see patients that would otherwise be unseen.

And please don't think you're being short-changed if you get allocated a locum in your next visit to the doctors. There truly is evidence that we can work wonders. It's because we're the fresh pair of eyes that some patients really need. Yes, there's a lot to be said for continuity of care. If you see the same GP for years and years then he or she should almost be able to antici-pate your needs. But what if that anticipation means they miss something? If old Mrs Blackstone always shuffles in breathing heavily and talking about her angina then you might be ready for your usual chat about a change in the beta blockers that slow down her heart and help it fill better. And in the process you might not spot that she's got a bit of a problem somewhere else.

A locum, who's never met the patient before, might see that while she's talking about her beta blockers her hand keeps moving up towards her neck, for example. A neck she's covering up with an odd-looking, high collared blouse. And what could be happening on her neck? I had a patient a while ago who answers the question. She was getting the very first signs of goitre, the old Derbyshire Neck that comes from iodine deficiency. They spotted this first of all in Derbyshire, hence the name. Derbyshire is one of the furthest places from the sea in the UK. So the people there used to get all their salt from mines where you don't get the iodine you get in the sea salt that's consumed by almost everyone else. These Derbyshire people developed growths on the neck – goitres. Check out the next packet of salt you see. It will probably make a point of its iodine content.

But back to being a locum. As the fresh pair of eyes we might spot the things that familiarity might miss. In a case like this we can ask our Mrs Blackstone the questions to make sure her thyroid gets the regulation it needs and the high-collared blouses can go back in the wardrobe. There are no guarantees, of course. Mrs Blackstone might be there for the angina as normal. But this is just a long-winded way of asking you not to write off a locum just because you've never seen us before. And don't just take my word for it. Researchers at the University of Bristol just ran through some 18,500 patient files. They found that 'a fresh pair of eyes' led to faster cancer diagnoses and faster follow-up appointments. People who turned out to have bowel or lung cancer were most likely to be diagnosed faster when they saw a new doctor rather than their regular GP. 'There seems little to be gained by waiting to see your usual doctor,' the report author said – a nice vote of confidence in us locums. So please don't feel bad if you're sent in to see one of us. Feel confident instead.

But, moving on to the nitty gritty of locum life. The surgeries where locums work all take a different approach to our services. Some send us all the one-off, unusual and infrequent visitors. Some send us all the regulars who hog too many of the appointment slots. Most send us the ones they know the regular doctors won't want. It means we see a different side of the NHS. We see the good, the bad, the ugly – and the downright annoying.

Or at least I do, today.

The first example is the patient who looks to be in her late fifties. She seems hale and hearty, striding across the room like a woman with a mission. Which is just what she proves to be.

'My daughter has got West Nile virus,' she declares with assurance as she sits down. She has her phone in her hand and a determined expression on her face.

'And your daughter is?' I begin.

'She's Jay. She's in Africa. She's working for some ridiculous third world charity no-one has ever heard of. She's teaching.'

'And she's been diagnosed with West Nile virus?'

Her mother waves a hand to dismiss such minor details as diagnosis. 'I *know* she has West Nile virus. She told me she's been feeling really tired. She's had headaches as well.'

I pause for just a moment. I'm not sure whose time is being wasted the most right now. I too feel tired, all of a sudden. I think I could have a headache coming on. But I doubt I've got West Nile Virus.

'You can speak to her now,' the woman's mother says before I can open my mouth to speak. And before I can object she has made the call.

'Darling, I'm at the doctor's surgery now. He's only a locum I'm afraid,' she says dismissively, not noticing or caring that I wince at her words. 'But you should listen to him. He's British, darling, he's British. He knows things.'

She passes me the phone. I take it, unwillingly. 'I'm Doctor Rudd,' I begin.

'I'm Jay and I'm so sorry to be disturbing you. My absolute nightmare of a mother is driving me bananas,' says a surprisingly deep voice on the other end of the line. It's a deep voice her mother can hardly fail to hear in my otherwise silent surgery. 'I've had a couple of mosquito bites, even though I do everything I can to avoid them. I googled West Nile Virus, just in passing. I know all about it and I know that I don't have it.'

I've wedged the phone between my shoulder and ear and I'm tapping at my screen to remind myself about a few more details of this disease. I'm aware, as I do so, that I'm probably doing nothing more than reading the same google page as her.

'Well, as you probably know, it is mosquito-borne. It is spreading a bit but in most cases it's something you're going to recover from. In most cases it sounds worse than it is.'

'I don't have it,' Jay repeats firmly.

'She's had a stiff neck. That's a text-book symptom,' interrupts her mother.

I ignore her. 'You've got medical staff you can speak to out there? And you are otherwise fit and healthy? No underlying health conditions I should know about?'

'Nothing at all. We've got great doctors here. They know I've not got West Nile Virus. I'm fine.'

'Well, I don't think there's anything else I need to say. Do you want to speak to your mother?' I ask.

'Not a chance,' she says flatly. The line goes dead.

I check my patient's name. 'Mrs Blanchflower, as you could probably hear, your daughter is perfectly fine and has plenty of people she can speak to there about any concerns she may have.'

'But my daughter needs proper treatment. I know what happens to people with untreated West Nile virus. She could be wiped out for the rest of her life. Her kidneys, her brain, her spine could all be affected. It's terrible. I've googled it,' she says.

Google, I feel, has a great deal to answer for.

'Well, all those things would be worst case scenarios if your daughter had got the condition and I don't think she does. I'm afraid there's nothing else I can do from here. And I do have a lot of patients waiting this afternoon. So if there's nothing else?'

I almost want to bite those words back as I say them. Being a GP brings one simple rule. Never ask if there's anything else. There almost always is. And you don't have time to deal with it.

Fortunately today is the exception to the rule. There isn't some other reason for the appointment. Mrs Blanchflower strides unwillingly out of the room.

My next patient, funnily enough, has also had a shot at self-diagnosis. But he's not been on the internet. He tells me he was on his way to the cinema in Leicester Square the other evening. On the way he walked through some of the back streets of Soho. He was a bit early. He had time on his hands. So he looked at a set of photographs of tongues in the window of a Chinese medicine shop. He didn't like what he saw. The pictures convinced him his spleen is a ticking time-bomb about to explode.

'Look at my tongue. It's covered in dots and grooves. There are lines on it too,' he begins.

I take a look. I can see what he means, but it really doesn't have anything it shouldn't have. Tongues are actually quite extraordinary things. They're small, really, but they've got more than half a dozen different muscles in them and they do more than we realise. Tasting, talking, cleaning our teeth, moving our food around – none of it's easy without a tongue, funnily enough. Most of the time we don't think about them. But oh how useful they are. And to be honest, how rarely do they go wrong. Yes, there are horrors. At the worst end of the scale there can be signs of oral cancer. Then there's so much else. So many fissures and spots and dots. Scarlet fever can show up on the tongue. There are even weird but mostly harmless things like geographic tongue, I seem to remember from medical school. And yes, on a less worrying note, mouth ulcers on your tongue can drive you mad for a while. Biting your tongue is not a lot of fun – and the wound you get when you do that can go a very funny colour before it heals. But it normally does heal.

This man's tongue does indeed have some grooves in it, but nothing that would bother me. I tell him he's winding himself up over nothing. I show him a very quick set of pictures on my screen to prove my point. I do a quick check on any other symptoms he might be feeling, of which there are none. So I send him on his way.

This, of course, is classic 'worried well' territory. People with odd little worries, ideas or fixations. They don't need medication. They need reassurance and sometimes just a healthy dose of reality. They certainly don't need dodgy pills from a side street in Soho.

As he leaves the room I can't help thinking of all the other, often even crazier reasons why people come to see us GPs. One of our associations has just done some research into it all. The results are fantastic – but not in a good way. They're shocking, terrible and awful in equal measure. But many of them are fantastically funny as well. When I get together with my doctor pals we pour over all our favourite stories. We run through some of the least believable of them – and then top them with stories of our own. The researchers, Resilient GPs I think they are called, have put them in several key categories, so show the craziest things member GPs have been asked about things which are really perfectly normal, about things which are utterly trivial, about administrative issues that should surely be dealt with elsewhere and about all the other madness that can't fit into any other sensible categorisation. Here are just a few of my current favourites. They're all from the first of the categories – the things which, really, should be seen as utterly normal.

'I went to the gym yesterday and now my arms are hurting,' is as good a place as any to start off with. Then there's: 'My skin is too soft.' And: 'I get sore feet when I dance in high heels.' Or how about: 'I'm allergic to cats. I'm getting a cat. Can I have a vaccination?' Or: 'My penis gets cold when I go outside' and 'I can't stop eating sweets and chocolate. I think I must have diabetes.'

I also love the ones where we get an explanation of what's really going on – though you don't really need a medical degree or to be a top detective to have worked them out. So how about: 'My son has a rash on his ankles every night' – and of course it's the mark from the elastic at the top of his socks.

Then there's the case of the woman who rocks up at her surgery and says: 'I'm worried about a white lump in my baby's gum.' The receptionist suggested it was a tooth. The irate mother said that only a fully, medically-qualified person could judge such a tricky diagnosis. She demanded an urgent appointment. It was indeed a tooth, the GP forum reports.

While I'm still thinking of all this I move on to the 'why on earth ask us?' questions GPs are faced with as well. Such as: 'Can you stop my twelve year-old daughter from just eating chips and pizza at dinner?' And then there are the downright 'out there' ones. Despite myself – and I feel for the poor kid involved - I like the one that goes: 'What normal fifteen-year-old boy doesn't have porn on his computer? I've looked and looked but he really doesn't. That's not normal.'

Back in the here and now I put all the funny stories aside and click through my next set of patients. I briefly practice my Spanish on one patient, I try a little faltering Portuguese on another and struggle with a third accent I can't pinpoint and can barely understand. This really can feel like the International Health Service at times. I then see a dear old lady whose ears are so blocked she can barely hear and an otherwise model-like twenty-something lady whose face has suddenly become plagued by adult acne or rosacea. There are tears from a middle-aged man who has lost his job and says he has lost his way in life. There are lots of forms to fill in and plenty of referrals to make. But it's a calm and pleasant surgery. And it throws up a difficult dilemma for my final patient, right at the end.

Chapter Six: Up in the Air.

THE lady who walks in to my final surgery of the day is beautiful. There's no way around that clear and simple fact. She's got all the 'T's' – a great tan, is perfectly toned and smiles with incredible pure white teeth. Plus any other 'T's' anyone can think of. But seriously she could hardly look healthier. She's tall (another 'T' I suppose) and casually dressed, her blond hair tied up in a pony-tail (almost another 'T', what's going on?) to make her look even sportier. If there's anything negative at all about her I'd say she looks as if she's wearing just a little too much make-up, especially for the time of day. But as GPs know, make-up can hide a multitude of worries, so I may get an explanation for that quite soon.

'And what can I do for you?' I say, as she sits down.

There's a slight silence as she gathers her thoughts. She seems to be holding herself together quite tightly.

'Is everything I say in here confidential?' she asks, her eyes locking on to the computer on my desk.

'Of course it is. It's entirely between you and me. Your medical records go nowhere,' I begin.

'But there are records? You take notes? Could other people see them? Do they go to my work?'

Her soft eyes are wider and wilder now. This bothers her. I run through a brief explanation of how patient confidentiality works. But she's not really listening.

'It can't go to my work,' she says. Then she adds something unexpected. 'Can I open the door?' Her head motions towards the surgery door that closed behind her.

'Of course,' I say. We always offer chaperones when patients want one, especially for personal examinations. But we've got no signs yet that any examination is going to take place. Interesting.

She opens the door, leaves it half way ajar and seems to visibly relax. Then she says the next line that surprises me. 'I need to see a psychiatrist,' she says.

'OK. And what sort of things do you want to talk to them about?'

Her eyes flash back to the half open door. 'I'm getting a bit scared, sometimes,' she begins. I hold back, waiting for her to elaborate. Like most doctors I've got a pretty good bullshit detector. Every day we face the fakers and the frauds who want to be signed off work or get some other golden ticket excuse provided for them. We've all dealt with people whose acting skills could make them a fortune, if they could only be bothered to learn any lines or do any work. So is this lady acting? I'm not sure. But I'm giving her the benefit of the doubt, of course. I need to hear more.

'It's difficult,' she says, falteringly. 'Sometimes I'm fine. I always used to be fine. But I don't seem to like being inside,' she continues. 'I don't like it when the doors are closed. I've got this stupid fear that I might be trapped. I need to know I can get out.'

'OK. And have you been feeling this for a while?'

'It's been building up. They're panic attacks, I know that. But I'm struggling to control them. I keep feeling that the walls are coming in on me. I feel as if I can't breathe, as if I'm going to suffocate.' There's a slight pause. 'It's worse at work,' she says.

'OK. And what job do you do?' I ask.

She gives a rueful look I don't understand till she speaks. 'I'm cabin crew. I'm a flight attendant,' she says. Of course she is. That explains her whole looks. The tan, the tone, the teeth and all the rest. She's one of those people who was born to do the job she does. But not, if she's truly afraid of small spaces.

'That can't be easy if you feel trapped,' I offer.

She grabs at my words. 'It's a nightmare, she says. 'I've had passengers over the years who are afraid of flying and they always say it's claustrophobia. I've never understood it. But now it's happening to me.'

'And you're still flying? You still go to work?'

'I do. But I'm sick, physically sick before and after the flights. And in the middle of them. When I'm in that metal tube on the tarmac, when the doors are shut and everyone is looking at me I've got nothing left to give. I don't know how much longer I can face it all.'

'OK, well we can work something out to try and sort this for you,' I begin. But there's a little more to come.

'And I've stopped going out as well,' she blurts out. 'I don't like it when I don't know what's going to happen. So I try to stay at home. Even getting here was horrible. I hated waiting in the waiting room. I hate this room here. I don't know what's happening to me. I don't know why it's happening. I'm a normal, ordinary person. I've done everything. I've travelled the whole world. I've had so many friends. And suddenly I'm falling apart.'

That's why there's so much make-up, I think as she rocks slightly in her chair. She's hiding what all this is doing to her face.

'And you've not mentioned it to anyone at work?' I begin, getting to the end of my need-to-know questions.

She answers fiercely. 'They can't know. They'll ground me. We can't have crew with mental issues. You can't tell them. That's what I'm so terrified about. I can't lose my job. I love my job. I'm just struggling to do it. But a psychiatrist can help. I know the right person can sort this out. They can? Can't they?' she begs.

'Of course they can,' I say firmly. 'You made it here today and you are still working so you're in a stronger position than you know. We can talk just a little longer here, and then I can think about finding people who can help you find long term ways to tackle this.' I ask more questions, assess more answers and run through anything else that could be going on in her body or her mind. Claustrophobia and panic attacks aren't as unusual as she might think. And if you're going to suffer from them then flying has to be one of the worst jobs you can do. But there's one other thing she said that struck me. She's stopped going out. She tries to stay at home. She doesn't like it when she doesn't know what might happen. I ask for a bit more information.

'When I get home from a flight I just lock the door and I feel safe.'

'And what about friends, partners, family? Do you have a social life still, do people come round?'

Her eyes fall. 'I've sort of dropped out. I can't face it so I find some excuse. Until my next flight I stay indoors.'

'What about food? How do you do your shopping?'

'Online,' she says. 'It's fantastic. I can order it when I'm away. It arrives when I'm back and I only have to open the door and it's done.'

'But if you wanted a pint of milk or a newspaper? Would you go down to the corner shop for them?'

She looks down again and thinks hard about this simplest of scenarios. 'I don't think I would,' she concludes. 'I'd do without. I'd rather stay at home.'

I tap a few words on to her file then I stop. I can tell this spooks her out. There's a mix in what she's said. A mix between claustrophobia where she can't cope with small spaces, and of agoraphobia where she can't be outside either. Is she making it all up? Is she bluffing when she says this can't go on her record or get to her employer? Does she want them to be told this story, so she can be signed off, probably on full pay? It's a tough one. And I'm mindful of the fact that her job carries responsibilities and safety issues. 'When is your next flight?' I ask.

'I've been signed off for personal reasons so I don't fly for ten days. I came up with a story. After that I'm going to have to come up with another one.'

'Well, I'll get you to talk to someone who can help before then,' I promise, crossing my virtual fingers as I speak and wondering what the wait times will be like in this part of London. I run though some information she can get online and some other places she can contact for help. She leaves the surgery, looking as good now as she did when she walked in. No-one seeing her in the street would guess there's a storm brewing in her mind. You'd think she had it all. It just goes to show you.

Chapter Seven: Bouncing Babies and Hidden Moles.

Another day, another new surgery. The room is hot and bright as I look at the clock on the wall. It's just gone quarter past ten. Probably a bit too early to head to reception to try and cadge a cup of coffee and a few biscuits. And talking of time – how am I doing? I've lost track of the number of patients I've seen so far this morning. I'm not sure if I'm ahead of schedule – well, actually, I do know that. Because GPs are never ahead of schedule. What I mean, is I don't know how far behind schedule I might be. And I'm not sure how much that might matter.

A weird little problem with being a locum GP is that you don't really know who you're there to impress. Obviously you want to put patient care at the top of your list. But you need to make a living as well. We all want to be asked back. But how to do so? We can listen endlessly to our patients' problems. We can empathise and commiserate and maybe even help out. Our attention-starved patients may pour their hearts out at great length and leave our surgery saying we're the best doctors they've ever seen. And maybe, just maybe, some practices will like that.

But I'd say most prefer someone who cuts out the chat, keeps to time, gets through their whole list by the end of the session and keeps the waiting area as empty as possible.

Time management is the vital skill they don't really teach at medical school. Anyway, it's all so random. You can't choose when the quick patients will come and when the time consuming ones will walk in. In a perfect world I like lots of quick people early in the day. That way the practice manager and the other partners to see me get the job done efficiently and quickly and get a great first impression. After that, later in the morning or the afternoon, I can fall behind with the more complicated cases. That's the perfect scenario. The NHS, however, is far from perfect.

I click to call in my next patient. It's a young mum and a baby. GPs surgeries are dominated by the diverse ends of the age range. We see more babies and old people than almost any other types of patient. And babies, of course, can be challenging. Most of the time – almost all of the time I'm pleased to say – crying is just crying, for example. But one case in 100 can be meningitis or something else that's serious. One case in a lot more than 100 can be some form of abuse. So you do need to keep yourself alert. These are things you cannot miss.

Today the first of my mum and baby combos gets off to a bad start. 'What's your baby called?' I ask, looking at an androgynous-looking bundle in a green baby gro.

'Taylor,' I'm told.

'And how old is she?'

'He's a boy,' I'm told angrily. With the subtext that if I can't work that out I'm unlikely to solve any other problems either.

'Of course he is,' I say. 'Fine looking young lad. Taylor. And what's his problem?'

'It's his face. Can't you see it?' There's an even stronger, accusatory tone in her voice now. This mum really does think I'm useless.

I look closer at little Taylor's face. He's got a wealth of those little white dots all around his nose and down to his mouth. They're incredibly common and perfectly normal, which, in my defence, is why I'd not even given them much thought when he came in. But they can be very disturbing for new parents – which is why Taylor's mum is so on edge.

'They're called Milia. They're really, really common in babies. They show up round the nose, just like this, and in other places as well. They're just a part of development. They're normal. Taylor is fine.'

'But they look terrible. They look like an illness.'

'They don't even hurt. Taylor won't even know they're there. They won't be bothering him at all,' I say. 'Ask any of the other mums you meet, they'll probably have seen them themselves. Are you in touch with any of your NCT group, or do you have other parents you spend time with?'

The woman shakes her head, put off balance and seemingly a little affronted by my question. 'Stuck up cows, most of the others,' she declares. 'I couldn't get away from them quick enough. I'm on my own with Taylor. It suits us.'

But not entirely, I want to say. The fact that you're here suggests that isolation is getting to you – and that you've less useful support than you might need. I try to explain it, as tactfully as I can. I try to say where this mum could meet other new parents, and hopefully not stuck up cows. I give Taylor a quick once-over and tell her that he really is doing fine. But I'm not sure she likes me. I'm not sure what the male equivalent of a stuck up cow might be. But in her eyes, I'm pretty sure that I'm it.

It's funny how things seem to come in patterns when you're a doctor. You might not see something for ages, then it crops up time and again. We get daily clusters too. I sometimes think I'm working Mental Health Monday, Tearful Tuesday, Worried-Well Wednesday or whatever it might be.

And this is bouncing baby Thursday, which I admit doesn't trip off the tongue quite as well.

My next baby turns out to be a very boisterous one. Jake, he's called, so even I can't make a second gender faux pas.

'We need to go to California next month,' his fragrant and expensively-dressed mum says proudly. 'I just wanted to be sure it's OK to take him. He's so young. I know people fly with new-borns sometimes. But I'm worried about the cabin pressure and all of that. Should we go?'

I'm smiling, despite myself, as I lean forward to give little Jake the once over. I like the way she said they 'need to go' to California the way I might 'need to go' to Tesco. What different lives we all lead. In a matter of minutes I've realised that Jake is good to go and very fit to fly. He's clearly thriving and has a strong pair of lungs on him – as demonstrated by his decibel-defying screams when he's first woken up and moved. But that's perfectly normal. His mum is confident, capable and knows what she's doing. I run through all the usual guff about protecting his ears and dealing with dry air

44

and possible motion sickness and the like. She's way ahead of me on all of it.

'So have a great trip,' I say as she wheels him out in his madly expensive buggy. And good luck to the people sitting next to you on the plane. Those little lungs will only get more powerful. That flight to California could be a very long twelve hours.

After a few regular patients and some nice and easy repeat prescriptions come next. Then there's a little bit of sadness. I'm seeing a middle aged lady whose elderly dad has just died. She's struggling with it. She's finding it hard to be alone in the world, even though they hadn't lived in the same house. She's struggling with guilt, feeling that she should have done and said more while he was with us. She's not unwell in any physical way. She's not in that bad a place mentally. But she needs someone to talk to. I wish, like all doctors, that I could give her more than a few, brief minutes. But time has been passing and my session is drawing to its close. I come up with the usual platitudes that I hope may still help. I pass on lots of places she can go to for support and advice. I tell her that her dad wouldn't want her to dwell on all of this. I get a weary smile of thanks as she leaves. I hope I've helped, just a bit.

When she leaves I grab a quick coffee from the reception area and take it back into my room. I call in my next patient. It's a man in his thirties.

'I'm worried about moles,' he begins as he sits down.

At which point I am always so very tempted to say: 'In your garden? Ruin the lawn, don't they?'

Instead, of course, I stay professional. 'I can take a look at them for you. Any ones in particular giving you cause for concern?' What I'll be looking at is the very long-winded

ABCDE of activity. We've all got moles, all over us. The vast majority are simply part of who and what we are. The ones that could be an issue are the ones that are 'asymmetric' for the A, have 'border changes' for the B, have shown 'colour change' for the C, and have big 'diameters' for the D as the larger they are the more worrying they could be, and lastly are 'evolving' for the E, which normally means ones that are itching, bleeding or changing in some other way.

'I've always had them on my arms, at the top, and on my shoulders. But I think there's more now than there used to be. I'm sure there are. And I can't see my own back. I don't know what's there.'

'Then let's take a look,' I say. He pulls off his sweatshirt and t-shirt. I look around the whole of his arms, including the underside. Then round his shoulders and his back. Nothing looks untoward, nothing abnormal. I take a moment longer looking at a greater mass of them on the back of his neck, looking up behind and around his ears as well. Nothing that stands out.

'I've got another one,' he says, not pulling his clothes back on when I give him what I'd thought would be good news. 'It's down here.' He motions to his groin. I don't know why, but my usual sixth sense had told me the arms, shoulders and back were just the smokescreen.

'Then let me see,' I say. And with a curious mixture of embarrassment and pride he starts to unbutton his jeans. As he does so, I'm reminded of an infamous old doctor everyone talked about back at my medical school. He was eighty, if he was a day. His surgery room was upstairs – and towards the end of his time he had to be practically carried up there at the start of each day and installed in a chair that was effectively his throne. When men came in, any men, of almost any age and for any reason, his initial response would be the same. 'And what have you come to see me about this time? Is it your John Thomas?' he would boom.

That said, I seem to remember his patients didn't just forgive him, they loved him. He was always happy to refer people to the experts they really wanted to see. And there had been a sense that he had seen it all and could spot what mattered and what was just froth.

Here, today, my patient's John Thomas (and I do keep meaning to look up where that phrase comes from because I bet there is a good story behind it) is ready to be examined. Again, he's displaying a curious mixture of embarrassment and enjoyment. GPs see our fair share of exhibitionism, from both sexes, over the years. Is this man really worried about anything, or does he just want a quick thrill, a chance to get naked in public and all paid for by the good old NHS? 'There, can you see it?' he says, focusing on what looks to be a skin tag on his scrotum. So there is something there. He's not making it up entirely. I check it out a little more and then get him to pull his jeans back up, which again seems to take longer than it should. I explain a little bit about what a skin tag is. They're those little brown or flesh-coloured things that hand off us like, well, tags. 'They're harmless, unless they're causing any real discomfort,' I tell him.

'But can I get rid of it?'

'They can normally be burned or frozen off. But I don't think we can do it here,' I say. 'It's not an NHS thing. You'll probably need to see a private doctor, and you will have to pay.'

'A private doctor,' he muses. Oddly he seems to quite like

the idea of seeing one of those. And he repeats it as he leaves the room. 'I'll go and see a private doctor about it.'

How very odd, I'm thinking as I tap in a few details on his notes. But how very great that his whole appointment, including writing up his notes, has taken less than six minutes. I'm on a roll. And for once I stay that way. Mr Moles is followed by a case of chronic bronchitis that's not been responding to the first burst of medication but should be sorted after a few tweaks.

Then there's a quick rectal exam for a man who is worried about his prostate now he's hit his late fifties. There's a little bit of measuring of blood pressure and trying to fill in the right forms to say I'm successfully counselling people about their weight and stopping them from smoking, when I suspect that all I'm really doing is helping the surgery to hit some targets and collect some extra cash.

My day ends with a whole slew of patients who want forms signing to get them off work – mainly for vague, unspecified 'pains'. I try to be tougher than some on these. I always think of the time I broke my leg skiing. I didn't miss a single surgery when I got back. I dragged myself around and I carried on doing my job – not because I'm a hero or a masochist but because that's what I was brought up to do. So tell me you can't go to nice warm and dry air-conditioned office because your leg 'hurts' and you'll get a proper physical examination just in case there's a sinister, serious reason behind it. But if there's nothing you won't get my signature.

Chapter Eight: Back to Hospital.

AFTER ten days spreading myself around a bit and working in five different rooms in four different surgeries I'm back in one of my old stamping grounds. I'm in a central London hospital. I'm doing a GP shift in an A&E department. Everyone knows the pressure Accident & Emergency is under. We know how hard the NHS is trying to close it down to everything except, well, accidents and emergencies. 'A&E won't kiss it better' is one of the best advertising lines about all that. But it isn't working. As we all know, A&E attendance keeps going through the hospital roof. And as so many of the patients would be better off seeing a GP then that's why some departments have GPs on offer.

We're there to try and weed out the timewasters and keep the main A&E cubicles free for the cases they're designed for. We're juggling a bit in this role. We need to be good. But we shouldn't be too good – because of course we don't actually want patients to leave A&E thinking they got exactly what they wanted and should now sidestep their usual GP for good.

More interesting for us doctors is the range of patients we're likely to see in hospital grounds. They should be one-offs. They can be real challenges.

Or, like the first one to walk through my door this afternoon, they can be textbook examples of why the NHS is in crisis.

The minute I see the man I guess what he's here for. But I have to hold back, just in case it's something else. You can never assume anything when you're a doctor. When I'd been training at my original teaching hospital I'd had a great senior physician, the professor of medicine who'd taken charge of what we call Grand Rounds. They're the weekly sessions for students and medical staff of all levels. We all get together to be told something about an unusual case that's just come into the hospital, about some new research or development, or about some speciality area that's useful to know about but which we might otherwise have missed. They're an amazingly useful ritual. And with the right leader they can be entertaining as well as hugely useful. My Grand Rounds man had been a true character. He had been full of life and full of great phrases. 'To Assume makes an Ass out of U and Me' had been one of his favourites. He had boomed the words out in a rich, fruity accent as he defied us to miss something, to make a false assumption and so make a mistake in a diagnosis. So I won't make an assumption with today's case, just yet.

My patient is a smart-suited man I'd place in his mid-forties. He's carrying a cycle helmet and a high visibility jacket as well as a panier and a computer case. But what draws attention is the fact that the left side of his face looks to have drooped dramatically. His left eye is almost completely closed, he is dribbling a little and as he tries to make a greeting only half of his forehead seems able to move. This man could, of course, be here because he has a verruca on his little finger or a great big boil on his bottom. Or he could, as I'm 99 per cent certain, be here because he has just developed Bell's Palsy.

'What can I do for you?' I ask.

'It's my face,' he says, spitting now, dribbling a little more and struggling to blink. He's slurred those three words and has an even more rueful, embarrassed look on his lopsided face.

'And when did this come on?'

'Probably yesterday afternoon. I started to feel a bit fuzzy, but thought it might just be the cold on my face, somehow. I cycle everywhere. It was cold yesterday. I thought I'd got a chill, maybe.'

'And what happened next?'

'I was worse when I got up today. I felt fine in myself. But my face – something was wrong. It was like I was numb from the dentist. I struggled eating my breakfast. It felt weird. But I thought maybe I'd just been lying funny in bed. I thought my face would wake up. But it got worse. I got through the morning. But then I saw myself in the mirror in the toilet at work. I knew it was something worse.'

'And have you seen your own GP?' I ask.

I get a grimace and another rueful, lopsided smile. 'I tried,' he says. He's really spiting and slurring now. All this talk is a real problem for him. 'I did call at nine this morning when it started to get worse. Then I called again at lunchtime when it was getting really worried.'

'Did you see them?'

He looks angry. His words are bitter. 'They said that because I'd not called at eight I wouldn't get an appointment.'

'Not even as an emergency?'

'Not even. I couldn't book for tomorrow either. They said I had to call at eight tomorrow to try and get an appointment then.'

'So you've come here,' I say.

He shakes his head. 'No. I went to the walk-in centre in Soho. They were good. The practise nurse said it was one of the worst cases of Bell's Palsy she had ever seen. She said I needed to take steroids within 72 hours to give it a better chance of a proper recovery. But she said they couldn't do a prescription for them there as I needed it done from my usual GP. She rang the surgery while I was sitting next to her. She said she was the senior practise nurse at the Soho NHS walk-in centre and she said they had to see me that afternoon to provide the prescription in time.'

'And they said no?'

'They said no and were really, really rude to her. She said the window for the steroids would end tomorrow morning so they had to agree to see me first thing tomorrow morning. The woman at my surgery said no. She just told her I had to ring at eight o'clock tomorrow morning and try my luck like everyone else. Then she practically hung up on her. The nurse said she'd never heard a surgery staff so rude. She said I should make an official complaint. And that I should come here.'

'Which surgery was it?' I ask. I'm wondering if I've worked there. Though to be honest it sounds like far too many places I've worked in recent years.

He tells me. I don't actually know it and I file the name away so I can hopefully avoid it. But I know I won't be able to avoid places like it. There's a growing trend to get rid of advance appointments all-together. A small but growing number of surgeries are introducing 'on the day only' deals.

You can't plan for important but non-urgent things on a day off from work that you'll book once you've got an appointment. Instead you need to book the day off work anyway, ring up in the morning and hope you get a slot. Will that work? Should it happen? I couldn't possibly comment. Though of course I'd like to.

Anyway, back to my Bell's Palsy patient. 'Let's get to business,' I tell him. I ask a few questions about his overall health which seems fine. I take a look at his face, his head, neck and the inside of his ears. There's an outside chance the signs of Bell's Palsy could be something like a stroke, a tumour or the result of some kind of head injury. But I don't think any of this applies today.

I tell the man what I gather he already knows. That this kind of thing can happen to almost any of us at any time. We don't actually know for sure when or why it will happen. There are factors that can make it more or less likely and more or less severe. But really it's just a case of minimising the symptoms and waiting for recovery to come.

'I'll prescribe you the steroids. They'll help reduce the swelling. There's no guarantee that they'll help enormously with your recovery. But the walk-in people were right that the sooner you start taking them the better.'

I take another look at his eyes before he goes. A side effect of the paralysis makes it hard to blink – and your affected eye can get dangerously dry. 'Have you been using eye-drops?' I ask and recommend them. I tell him he might need to tape his eye shut at night, so it doesn't dry out while he sleeps as well.

'And do I need to come back here?' he asks when he's taken it all on board.

'I should tell you to see your own GP to report all this to them,' I begin. He splutters and dribbles a bit at the mention of his GP. 'But really with Bell's Palsy it's just about taking the time to recover. The steroids should help. But the disease does just run its course. People I've seen in the past say it seems to go almost as quickly as it comes on. Worst case scenario is that it can last for six to nine months. But most of the people I've seen find it goes much sooner. Often around the six week mark. The good news is that it shouldn't get any worse. And if it doesn't get better at that point then you may want to come in just to be sure. But, really, just take the medication straight way, watch out for your eye and wait.'

I hand him the prescription and a few print-outs I've made on the illness and its progression and watch him leave. The story about his normal GP still bothers me far more than his sudden illness. We can't get everything right in the NHS. But there is such a fine line between the frequent fliers who over-use the service and turn up with ridiculously trivial or imagined illnesses and the genuinely ill who don't get a timely diagnosis because they can't get through their surgery's door.

We all know about the pressure to get appointments. We all read the surveys about the people who've given up trying and pitch up here, at A&E because they think – or know – that it's the one place they'll get seen. So that's why I'm here, today, in a room alongside an A&E department, to try to square this horrible circle. I'm here to triage people and take the pressure of the A&E guys. But by being here I'm also confirming to people that it makes sense to rock up at hospital rather than to wait at their local surgery. How will it all end? With a Whitehall re-organisation, I'd imagine. Will that help? No comment.

Chapter Nine: Silly Stories.

A middle-aged woman comes in and irritates me before she has made it half way across my small surgery. She's carrying a giant Starbucks cup of coffee. So, you want a free GP's appointment as part of your free NHS. You probably want a strong police force and a good fire brigade. You want decent benefits and pensions. I'm sure you want a good, free education for your children. But you choose to buy your expensive coffee from a foreign company that could have helped fund all this by declaring profits and paying corporation tax. Instead, though, for all the coffee it has sold the company has paid next to no corporation tax in, what, fifteen years? How, exactly do you expect that all to work? I detest hypocrisy. I will never buy my coffee from Starbucks. To me it will always be a company for teenagers, tourists and tax cheats. And for this smug-looking lady who I'd rather not have to meet.

I give her the briefest of fake, half-smiles. 'So, what can I do for you?' I ask with minimal eye contact.

'I've hurt my back,' she says. I'm even less interested now and if anything my bad mood has got worse. Back pain is bread and butter stuff for GPs. We hear about it all the time. And there's never much we can do.

'Tell me more about it,' I prompt. Still no real eye contact. Her coffee smells sickly and sweet.

'I was picking up the children's clothes. I must have twisted myself, somehow. I was in agony. I had to stay on the ground for a good ten minutes before I could get up. Then I needed another ten minutes when I finally managed to get into a chair.'

'When was this?'

'Two days ago.'

'And how is your back now?'

'It still aches. It's sensitive. I can feel it.'

'And have you taken any anti-inflamatories to calm it down?' She looks outraged. 'No. I don't take things like that. I didn't want to just mask the pain, I want to treat it,' she says, self-importantly.

I sigh. 'Anti-inflamatories don't just mask the pain,' I begin. 'They do what they say. They reduce the inflammation. And it's likely to be the inflammation that is causing the pain.'

'But inflammation is the way the body protects you from an injury,' she declares, spouting out spurious 'facts' with a lifetime of self-confidence. 'Inflammation swells up to protect the damaged muscle. So if you get rid of the inflammation you make the damage even worse. Everyone knows that.'

I sigh again. I try to explain that everyone can be wrong. I run through what could really be going on inside this annoying lady's back. I run through the exercises she should consider, tell her that the best thing to do is to keep moving and to try and carry on as normal. Taking to your bed with a bad back is one of the worst things to do. Though I sort of wish this lady had taken to hers and not rocked up here. With her vast bucket of crap coffee.

Half a dozen or so patients on and I'm out of the office for a while. I'm doing some unexpected house calls as the surgery staff juggle around everyone's work load. I see some of the worrying sick patients, the ones needing palliative care as their end approaches. I talk to some brave, kind, sad and scared family members. I start some paperwork after one expected death. I feel a little down.

But I can pick myself up. I have to. Because one of the very many things I love about medicine and being a doctor is the fact that our days can swing so fast from happy to sad and from joy to tragedy. So, after the shadow of death in the afternoon, I sit on the tube heading home and read through some of the other 'craziest things' that other GPs have dealt with. Trust me, they're genuine. Here are some of my other favourites.

'My poo smells this morning and it doesn't normally.' Said with said excrement wrapped in tinfoil in a plastic bag. Plus: 'Can you fix my sprained ankle before I go out tonight as I want to wear high heels.' Or the patient who turned up wanting help because: 'I burned the top of my mouth on a pizza five days ago.'

As you might imagine, anything to do with babies and children can be serious and important. Or it can be ridiculous and funny. So how about: 'My child has turned blue!' And funnily enough the child had been sleeping under a new, blue, duvet cover that hadn't been washed.

As it happens, the colour blue crops up quite often in our various surgeries. 'My three-year-old daughter's poo is bright blue. Look!' one colleague was told. And there it was, in a Tupperware tub the mum then produced. 'Has your daughter been doing any drawing with crayons lately?' the mum was asked. Yes she had. 'Then I suspect the blue one is missing,' mum was told. Still with babies, but changing colour, how about: 'My baby's snot is just too green.'

Next up on the list are a slew of things that patients ask to have prescribed – because for many people prescriptions are free. So people come in asking for sunscreen, toothpaste, shampoo ('to make my hair shiny') chap-stick ('because my lips are chapped') plus, my favourite, 'I want a prescription for everything I need from the chemist, including nappies, toothpaste, toilet roll and shampoo'.

What else do patients ask of us? A lot of admin for the things they actually want from other places. 'Can you write a letter for my housing department? Can you say the corridor is too narrow for two people to walk through it at once? I'll wait while you write it. I don't mind,' one patient said with a shameless amount of front and entitlement. Not that this is so unusual, especially when it comes to anything to do with housing. 'Can you write a letter to get me a new flat? Mine is really dirty,' one of the doctors had been told according to the researchers drawing up this latest list of mad medical requests.

Then there are all the questions that come to us, but which really ought to go to almost anyone else.

I carry on reading the latest report with a combination of horror and humour. I'm so engrossed I nearly miss my connection on the way home. I see that fellow doctors have faced like questions such as: 'Do you know how I can get into the furniture design business?' or 'We don't have the same travel channel on our cable TV as our neighbour. What are you going to do about it?' And you know what?

And we can't always just dismiss these sort of questions and suggest people find more suitable help elsewhere – because the patients can come back to haunt us. I love the tale of the patient who turned up at a surgery saying they can't decide whether or not he should move to Australia. The doctor, of course, said he couldn't really say. And so the patient put in an official complaint. Apparently the doctor was: 'A bloody useless GP. No help whatsoever.'

Chapter Ten: A Warmer Welcome.

OF COURSE one of the greatest things about being a locum – or a sessional or a freelance GP or whatever we all want to call ourselves - is that if we work with bad people one day we can move on the next. We don't have to face the same bad attitudes and useless faces day after day. Nor do we have to get to grips with the unique hell that is the NHS human resources department if you want to take the extraordinarily unwise step of trying to dismiss someone – however incompetent, or unsuitable they may be.

Instead you just move on to the next surgery and hope for a better time. That's what I'm doing today. And that's just what I get.

'Doctor Rudd, how marvellous that you're here. You're an angel to have come, an absolute angel. We've got a hideous backlog here. It is chaos, I'm afraid. And not even organised chaos, just pure, simple chaos. You look young, thank god. You'll need to be. It's going to be a long, hard day.'

But it's going to be a fun one, I decide. I already like the lady who's given me this warts-and-all welcome. She's probably in her early sixties. She's got short, thin, white hair and behind some very jazzily-framed spectacles she's got bright, lively eyes.

'My name is Sheila, by the way. I'm the practice manager and I'd guess from looking at you that I've been here for longer than you've been alive. We've got five doctors here. We're a good team. We get along, we help one another and we do our best for our patients. Let me tell you about the surgery and the rooms.' She rattles through a long laundry list of information about the facilities and the kit and I love it. It's amazing how rarely we're told the important stuff when we turn up at new surgeries. We don't need to know everything, to be fair. But if we're called upon to use an auroscope then it helps to know where it might be.

'Coffee?' Sheila asks as we arrive in the reception area. She points to a fancy looking espresso machine in the office. 'It's the most expensive and most useful bit of equipment we have in the whole practice. I'll make you a cup,' she says.

When I've got my brew I get introduced to the rest of the team, including two of the regular GPs who have come out of their rooms to greet me. I'm liking it even more when Sheila comes back into the room with a big brown file. 'It's the locum pack,' she says proudly. 'It's got everything you need to know, I hope. All the equipment we've got and where we keep it. Everything about the computers. All the phone numbers you'll need for referrals or blood tests and the procedures we have for results.' I grab it like a drowning man grabs a life raft. Locum packs, those rare and precious things, can be fantastic.

Sheila leaves me 'to settle' as she puts it. I'm smiling broadly. Every now and then locums like me are welcomed to new surgeries like heroes because the practice manager and the partners know we'll clear their waiting rooms, soak up all their most irritating and incoherent patients then disappear without adding a single drama to their on-going office politics.

My first patient today is a tired and distant looking gentleman who I learn is eighty two. He's thin and spare and smartly dressed in what looks to be the very best clobber that M&S sold many years ago. He's here because his hearing is getting worse and he needs – or should I say he wants – his ears to be syringed. He's also struggling to sleep, suffering with ever-increasing aches and pains and is worried about his prostate, his hips and his heart. But beyond the laundry list of small complaints I have to ask what could really be going on? I've only just met the man, of course. I've got barely five more minutes with him if I'm to keep to time. But I'd say the single, simple fact is that he's depressed. This man is getting older and he doesn't like it. He doesn't like the indignities and the inconveniences of feeling that his body has faded and that bits of it are starting to fail. The aches and pains may be in his head, just as much as in his bones. He's a widower, I learn. All of his grown-up family live far away. There are very few visits. He's lonely. More than that, and it's a small, underused word, he's sad.

What will help him? Getting out more, is my true diagnosis. Seeing other people of his own age or in fact of any age. Having a purpose, an interest, a reason to wake up and to get up each day. Loneliness is an extraordinary, invisible, intruder into our lives. It can switch so many of us into shut-down mode. It can creep up on you and seep right through you. It scares people. It drags them down. And it makes bad situations and bad health so much worse.

What surprises my non-doctor friends is that we see

loneliness hit people right across the age range. This dignified, older widower is a classic case. But his son, or possibly even his grandson could be feeling the same. Loneliness hits men as much, maybe even more, than it hits women. And isolation hits in big cities as well as in small villages. In fact it can be worse in places like London as it's so much easier to fall through the cracks and be ignored and forgotten when you're in plain sight in a crowd.

What can doctors offer the lonely, the sad and the genuinely and deeply depressed? For younger patients I'll be honest and say the kind of care you get will depend on where you live. That's one of the other things we're not supposed to address about the NHS. We all say we want local accountability, local control and local services for local people. Then we get them – and we complain about postcode lotteries where facilities decided upon and offered in one area aren't seen as priorities in others. Mental health services can fit right into this category. In some parts of London I know there are incredibly good talking therapy sessions on offer. Even more incredibly, you don't always sit on a waiting list forever when you try to access them. In other places, though, you do just see your name go on a list and you get forced to wait for far, far too long.

Do talking therapies work? They can, of course they can – and in many ways that's more to do with the listening than with the actual talking. It sounds a bit prim to say it's important to give someone a voice. But lonely people need a voice sometimes. Talking, listening and sharing really can help. But it's not what everyone wants, needs or gets. What huge numbers want, get or get given are anti-depressants. It's the medicalisation of our world and of course these are absolutely vital in all those extreme cases when people need to be taken back from the edge. What I don't like is dishing those out when people aren't at the edge at all. If someone is in front of me because they've faced a sudden life crisis then we do sometimes have to be cruel to be kind. Or clear, to be kind.

I had a guy in one of my surgeries recently. He was in his late twenties. He didn't think his life was working out. He couldn't get the job, let alone the career that he wanted. Friends were getting married and starting families. He was single, in a rented flat with neighbours who partied all night and stopped him from sleeping. None of that was great, of course. But none of it could be tackled by medication. So, terrible as it may sound, this is what I said to him.

'Life's shit. But it will get better. It normally does.'

I'd said it with as much of a smile, a shrug and a sense of realism as I could muster. It had been my genuine, gut feeling for what this patient had needed to hear. It's actually my gut feeling for so many people I see. It's the attitude that can see us through things. Shit happens. But life does, normally get better. 'At least you're not dead,' is what one of my fellow GPs tells some of her patients. I certainly can't say either of those things to my elderly patient today. But I still think there's an answer that won't involve medication and pills.

'How much do you get out and about?' I ask my older gentleman in conversational fashion as I prepare to race through the rest of his appointment.

He looks a bit affronted and a bit irritated. But he does reply. 'A little. But I've not much to go out for.'

'Well you know that on almost every level you'll feel better if you go for a walk every day, maybe just to buy the paper.

And maybe get a coffee and read it in a café rather than taking it home. It probably sounds silly. But things like that can help. When did you last sit in a café?'

This time my patient really does look at me as if I'm mad. 'Why?' he asks.

'Tell me,' I say, ignoring his question. 'When did you last sit in a café?'

He still looks appalled at my stupid question. But I want an answer. And in the end he gives in and supplies one. 'Never,' he says. 'Why would I do that? Noisy, full of people, all sitting there on their phones and screens. I wouldn't do it.'

'Well humour me, and do it today,' I tell him. 'Feel free to think I'm an idiot. Feel free to think I'm patronising you. But I'm not. I think you should get out more – and stay out more. Everything you've said suggests you spend all your time at home, on your own. I don't think that's healthy. If you really wanted it, I could give you the evidence to prove it. I'll come back to it later. But let me just check on those other things first.'

I ask the man a few questions as I do the roundabout checks to make sure that his other issues aren't anything serious. He was in the army, he says as I take a look in his ears. They're pretty much OK and tell him we should see syringing as a last resort a long way down the line. He had been based all around the world, he says, as I check his flexibility and his movements. He's had a grand old life, he says with a mix of pride and regret as I wind things up. I tell him he's actually in fine old shape. I give a few more possibly patronising platitudes about voluntary work and things he can do and organisations he can join to connect with his peers.

'And will you sit in a café and have a pot of tea this afternoon?' I ask as he gets ready to leave.

He gives the briefest of smiles. It's the first time his face has changed since he arrived. And the smile takes years – maybe decades - off him. 'I do think you're an idiot,' he says.

'You're probably not alone,' I offer. 'Just humour me.'

This time I get a real smile. And a nod that confers just a modicum of kindly respect. Then he's gone. And what else could I have done? You know what? If it was possible I'd have written this man a prescription for a dog. Not a wild and crazy puppy. A shaggy old dog needing a new home – maybe one whose previous owner has just passed away. An old dog and an old soldier would go well together. This gentleman should buy one. Then he'd take those walks around his neighbourhood. He would get that small amount of gentle physical exercise that we know can make a huge amount of psychological difference as well. He might say 'good morning' to a few people. He might chat to the occasional fellow dog-walker. He might sit in a café one sunny afternoon and feel glad to be alive.

Chapter Eleven: Moments of Sadness.

I'M IN London's East End today and it's a world away from my last surgery in a leafy suburb five or six miles north. The building itself is top notch. Lots and lots of money has been spent here. We've got a big, high reception area with glass ceilings, lots of toys for the kids in a vast play area, lots of indoor trees and plants, lots of colourful chairs to sit on. There are even a few comfy sofas. I'd quite like to live here, I think, as I give it the once over on my arrival. If I could afford it.

The patients, though, are nowhere near as colourful as their surroundings. Almost all the women in my East End waiting room are fully covered up. It's a sea of black. It could well be a sea of friendly faces, I think as I walk towards my room. But I have no way of knowing. I can't see anyone's face. I know so many people will hate me for even commenting on this. But it makes my heart sink a bit. It makes me think the day will be a bit depressing. I do medicine because I like people. I like helping people, talking to people and reading people. Of course I can help, talk to and read people whose faces are fully covered. But it's harder because sometimes we learn from visual as well as verbal clues. Sometimes we can read things on someone's face, we pick something up from what they show, rather than say.

Anyway, rant over, there's something else that's a little bit politically incorrect I might be able to say about today's surgery. It's that the last time I worked regularly in places with this atmosphere we seemed to get a lot of non-English speakers. That meant we had a lot of interpreters and translators on hand. The taxpayer in me didn't really approve of that. Nor did the social cohesion fan in me. But the GP in me? I loved it. Because generally speaking people who spoke no English and needed an interpreter got a double appointment – another thing that sometimes annoyed the taxpayer in me. But the GP? Double appointments are fantastic. With luck you can use them to claw back some time and catch up with your list. So bring them on.

Anyway, as it turns out we don't have any interpreters today – and if we'd needed them the surgery manager tells me we've got a phone translation system in place. It's something that drives most of us mad but it promises to cut overall NHS costs which has to be good.

Anyway, the other good news is that my black-clad patients are, of course, pretty much the same as everyone else. Whatever we wear we tend to have the same bodies, the same medical issues, the same concerns. It means the surgery runs almost exactly as normal. I talk a lot, write a lot of prescriptions and print out a lot of information sheets. Then I see something as I grab a chance to dash out of my room to get a refill of water from the machine in reception. Elizabeth, one of the older Ghanaian ladies behind the reception desk looks to be crying.

'Are you OK?' I ask, stopping alongside her.

'I'm fine, it's nothing,' she lies.

'You don't look fine. What's happened? Can I do anything?'

So she tells me. 'It's one of our old-timers. She was a soppy old dear. She only came in every now and then. She was never any trouble. She didn't abuse it. If she was here, it was important to her.'

'And has something happened?'

Elizabeth lets out a long, low sigh. 'It was her husband. He was here sometimes as well. He had a lot of chronic issues and he didn't walk all that well but he got by. They were a nice little couple. They would come together most times. They'd wait for each other. They were polite and respectful. They were nice. They said hello and they said goodbye. They said thank you. And so few of them say that. You notice the ones that do. You get to like them.'

I stand by and wait for what must be coming next.

'She called earlier on,' Elizabeth says. 'She said her husband had had a bit of a strain. She said he was in pain, on his side and on his back. We told her to give him some paracetamol and to call back in an hour if he'd not settled. He died in that hour. He had an aortic aneurism. We've just had the call to tell us. Her husband died. He was a dear, dear old man.'

I try to say a few words that might help, but it's not easy. And Elizabeth is still lost in her own thoughts. 'These old dears, they don't like to make a fuss,' she repeats, almost to herself. 'If she'd said a little more when she'd called we might have got him in, or got someone out to him. But it didn't sound serious. She said it was a strain. That's why we told her to give it an hour before calling back.'

'We'd not have been able to do anything in that hour,' I

say, watching a single tear form and then fall from Elizabeth's right eye.

'I know.' There's another tear now, falling from her other eye. 'I know it was his time. But I liked him and I liked her. I wish it hadn't happened like this.' She sighs, then looks up and gives me a defiant stare. 'At least it was quick, right? And our show has to go on. Patients are waiting, right doctor?' The tears have been wiped away. Her face is almost dry. She turns back to her computer and logs back into the system. This is a strong, capable and kind lady. Patients are waiting. And the show has to go on.

Chapter Twelve: Getting Down to Business.

THE admin that full-time GPs have to do scares the heck out of me. I'm not Alan Sugar or Richard Branson. I'm not a businessman and I don't want to pretend to know how to run a company. It's bad enough dealing with my own tax form every year. I don't want to worry about the cleaners' taxes, the receptionists' taxes, the practice manager's tax and all the rest of it.

Still, I could live without some of the insults. 'You locums, you're just a bunch of medical misfits,' one of my pals joked once. Or at least I hope he joked. I'm preparing to hear plenty more comments like that tonight. I'm catching up with a group of old pals from Med School. We'll be sitting round a big table in a bar near the London Eye. Several of my friends are now partners in GP practices, several are hospital consultants and some are going higher in ever-more specialised disciplines. All told we'll make a pretty capable table. If you're ever going to have a heart attack or a medical emergency in a bar then this is the one to choose. Whatever happens one of us will have you covered.

But back to my fellow GPs. The ones who've become partners. It's like they're speaking a different language, I think as we get our first round in. Or it's as if they're describing an entirely different profession. These guys really are Alan Sugar. All they talk about is money. What about the patients? Had any of them seen any particularly gruesome or interesting or exciting cases lately? That's what I want to ask. But they just want to talk about the cash. And, to be fair, it's not just about the money they have coming in. They just as obsessed by what's going out. They bore for Britain on the cost of, well, locum GPs like me.

'So where've you been working lately?' I'm asked amidst much speculation about my day rate.

I run through a list of surgeries, including a few I'd had to travel down towards the suburbs for – including one infamous suburb with a hospital that's had a very bad press.

'So you sent people to the Mayday hospital? The May Die hospital?' I'm asked when I mention the area I'd been to. We really should stop referring to it as that, I think. None of our jokes are good. But that one could get us into trouble.

'Every hospital is crap nowadays,' interrupts one of our grumpiest consultants. 'Stupid rules. Stupid managers. Swivel-eyed crazy politicians.'

'Bad day?' I ask him.

'Fed up,' he says. 'I used to be proud of my job. I wore a shirt and tie. I tried to be what people expected their consultant to be.'

'Ties went long ago,' he's reminded.

'Exactly. Infection risk. Ridiculous. Long sleeves have gone now. I have to wear a short sleeved shirt. I look like I work behind the desk in a car rental company. It's all politics. It's the dumbing down of medicine. They want everyone to dress alike. From the consultants to the cleaners. Would I want to be told I've got cancer from someone who dresses like a cleaner? Would that make me feel I'm getting professional care? Load of old cobblers.'

We let him moan on for a while. Then we go back to the conversations we all prefer. The stories of all the other crazy things that patients say and do. Almost all my colleagues have read the latest lists of time-wasters. We all particularly love: 'Doctor, I have toothache.' 'Have you seen your dentist?' 'No.' And the closely related issue of the patient who wanted to talk about the health of her guinea pig, and who wanted her GP to prescribe medication on the NHS as she didn't want to pay vets' bills.

Then there's the woman who came to ask her GP why there was one Viagra tablet missing from her husband's packet. And, possibly related, the patient who wanted their GP to help 'make' them diabetic – so they could qualify for free Viagra.

Add in the patient who wanted her GP to tell her partner to stop buying food that was near to the sell-by date – 'because it's wasting money'.

Then, as usual, we move on to the mad old days – though I suppose everything is relative.

'The surgery I'm covering for is a one-man band,' says Anil, one of my oldest pals. He's doing locum shifts way up in north east London. 'It's a very old man band. His wife runs the patient list. And do they have stories to tell. Their old surgery didn't have an examination couch, they told me. When they needed to use one they had to take patient across the road. They had to get a key from the greengrocer in the shop opposite. Then they went upstairs where there was some random room in a flat with a sofa they could use for a couch. But nothing else. They had to use soap for lube, she tells me very proudly. They used the same kit to look down someone's ears that they'd just used to look up someone else's bum. Good old days, right?'

We move on to a more modern tale. It's of the London locum who felt like a total break from city life and saw an advert for a short term relief posting way out on the islands of Scotland. The deal had his transport paid, and put him in what looked like a perfect little Bed & Breakfast by the port. The surgery was another one-man band, this time run by what sounded like a redoubtable female GP who had ruled the roost for years but was taking a two month break to go on an Alaskan cruise. On his first day the surgery receptionist cluttered around the London doctor, settling him into his consulting room before breaking the bad news about how busy the surgery would be.

'I'm sorry, doctor, but we don't have a single slot today for patients,' she had said.

'That's not a problem,' she had been told. 'Down in London I'm used to busy surgeries when all the slots are full. I'm happy to squeeze in any extra patients whenever I can and I'll happily stay late and see anyone else who's left at the end.'

He'd been given a blank stare. 'No, doctor, you don't understand. I don't have a single slot booked. There's no-one coming in to see you all day.'

How different the rest of our stories are that night. We all go on to talk of madly crowded, endlessly busy days. We moan like mad. But it's clear we love it. Doctors always do.

Chapter Thirteen: A Killer Cactus.

A YOUNG mum and her sheepish looking son are first in my room the next morning. 'It's his hand,' she begins, mercifully brief and to the point. I'm grateful because I've been told my normal list will have several additions to it so every second will count.

'Ouch, what did you do to get that?' I ask as the youngster opened up his right palm. His index finger is swollen, red and seems to be giving off enough heat to warm the room. There's a multi-coloured pinch point right on the pad of the finger which I'm guessing is the source.

'It was a cactus,' he says, a little bit embarrassed, but a whole lot proud.

'Attacked you, did it?' I ask.

'He wanted to take it out of the living room and up to his bedroom. He had the pot in one hand and grabbed the cactus itself with the other one. He screamed so loud the neighbours must have heard.'

'I dropped the cactus.'

'Made a big mess. Soil everywhere.'

'And it did some damage to your finger,' I say, stating the obvious.

'We tried to get all the spikes out but I don't think we did it,' explains his mum. 'He said he could still feel something sharp in his fingers the next day. Some of the spike must be almost invisible. Then it started to go septic. It went up like a balloon.'

And so it did. Septic is one of those words that's very often misused – but which everyone sort of understands when they hear it.

'Let's take a quick look,' I start. Fortunately I'm in a decent surgery today and most of the equipment works – which isn't always the case. I click on my pen torch so I can see if there are indeed spikes still embedded in the boy's fingers. The whole puncture wound is a bit of a mess so it's not easy to tell. This will take some serious cleaning. And there's a whole lot of puss building up that needs to be dealt with as well. Because that could make a bad job a lot worse.

'Rubor, calor, tumor and dolor,' I say, showing-off and trying to keep the lad interested as I carry on with the quick examination. 'They are the key signs of infection – in Latin. What do you think rubor is?'

'A ruby?' he asks, seeming genuinely interested.

'Close. Redness.'

'Rubies are red.'

'Exactly. And calor?'

'Dunno,' he says.

'Something like calor gas?' asks his mum.

'Sort of,' I say. 'It's heat. And tumour and dolor are swelling and pain.'

'Cool,' says the boy, improbably interested.

'Fingers are funny things,' I continue as I get ready for the next quick step I'll have to take. 'There's not a lot of room inside them for all the tendons and nerves and things inside them. And they're at the end of the line so if they get inflamed and swell up like this everything can back up and damage things with all the pressure. And you don't want to risk any problems with your index finger.'

'I'm left handed,' says the boy, clearly proud.

'You still need your other hand,' I tell him. So I get a sterile pin ready to bleed out some of the smelly yellow pus that the mum looks at in horror and the boy looks at with something approaching sheer joy.

'Disgusting,' she says.

'Cool,' he counters.

I smile as I do a quick referral to a hand surgeon – a bit over the top but important because he really could build up some problems if the infection builds up again. The pair of them collect their things and start to leave the room. But as they go the mum turns round and pays me one of the biggest complements a mum can pay to a GP. 'I think he wants to be a doctor himself now,' she says.

'Cool,' I hear myself reply.

My next notable patient is a mildly hysterical middle aged woman who has got the mildest bit of athlete's foot – for what she says is the first time in her life. She's convinced it will lead to blood poisoning (or a blood clot, she's unclear which). But she knows it will kill her. 'My husband said it was athlete's foot,' she admits grudgingly as I try to reassure her and move her on. 'He said he's had it in the past.' Those eight words sounded like an accusation. Her next words confirm it. 'Why would he have had athlete's foot?'

'You don't need to be an athlete,' I begin, wondering if this whole things is a wind-up.

'But who would he have caught it from? Could he be having an affair? I know he's having an affair.'

'Athlete's foot isn't a sexually transmitted disease.'

'So where did he get it? And where did I get it?'

'From gyms, from swimming pools, from all sorts of places. It can just happen,' I say, flailing just a little. I must admit I can't remember or maybe I never knew that much about mild athlete's foot. I've just seen it as something that exists. Something you don't need to worry about. 'Get some cream from the pharmacy when you leave,' I begin.

I'm interrupted. 'My husband had cream. In his gym bag. I knew nothing about it.'

I'm nonplussed. 'Well, it's not necessarily something you'd talk about a great deal. It isn't a big deal. It's just athlete's foot,' I repeat, feeling I'm letting things slip away from me here.

'Don't I need a prescription? Some pills? Antibiotics?' she asks.

'You really, really don't. Every chemist sells athlete's foot cream. You can buy it own-label. It will be cheap. Supermarkets sell it. It's that common.'

'I was about to go to A&E last night when I first saw it,' she says. 'I googled it and saw it could cause blood poisoning.'

Google again. And this has to be a joke now, right? 'I'm glad you didn't go to A&E,' I say firmly. 'Trust me, that's not something we should ever take there. It's accident and emergency, remember, and this isn't either – whatever google might throw up. Get some cream, follow the instructions, maybe use some talc too to keep your feet dry. It will clear up. It really is nothing.'

Grudgingly the woman pulls her shoes back on and leaves. She's shaking her head and muttering as she does so. It's hard to make out exactly what she's saying. But I think I catch the final few words she says as she leaves my surgery. 'I bet he's having an affair.'

Chapter Fourteen: So You Want to be a Perfect Patient?

WILL I carry on as a day-time locum? I keep asking myself the question. It's not as exciting as my old, night-time work. Doing all those 2am house calls across London was one of the most exciting times of my career. But it had been the most anti-social time as well – and at some point soon I would like to settle down and maybe even start a family. So day shifts have to be the way to go. Will I take on a full-time 'proper' job as a salaried GP or as a partner?

I know that in many ways it would be fantastic to do so. I like it when things work. And if I worked in the same room, at the same surgery, every day I'd make sure that everything does. In my perfect, full-time world I'd never run out of A4 paper. I'd never find that there's prescription paper in the printer when I want to write out a referral letter, or headed paper in there when I want to dash off a prescription.

But I'd miss the chance to see different areas and different types of patient every few days. With well over 1,000 people on your list you should always have a bit of everything. But in London you very often don't. Your catchment area is normally one thing or another. Posh or poor. Immigrant or indigenous. Even young or old.

I'll be honest, and admit I might lose out financially if I took a proper job as well. It's a buyers' market for GP locums right now. Rates are going up – though they're not quite the '£120,000 a year for GPs who just work weekends' deals that we read headlines about in the papers. I would, though, quite like annual leave and study leave to be built into my contracts so I can relax a little more and not have to do all the extra stuff in my own time.

It might also be nice to be a full time, same-place GP and to offer the continuity of care that patients actually want. I feel that today.

My patient is a hefty looking heavy-smoker of a man with a face that's lived a hard life.

'I'm here to get the results of my blood test,' he says, slumping down in the chair by my desk.

'OK, right, can you tell me when that was and what it was for?' I ask, scrolling down my screen to see what may or may not be in the man's notes. There's quite a lot, as it happens. But no mention of any outstanding bloods.

'And who requested it?' I ask as he fixes an accusatory glare on me.

'Doctor Petrucci? Or Petardo or something like that.'

'And when was it done?'

'About a month ago.'

'And why was it done?'

It turns out, of course, that the patient is tired all the

time – Tatt, as we say. And after a bit of digging I find the results – they're nothing that's really out of the ordinary but as they are mildly abnormal I do need to ask more questions. And they are probably the same questions he was asked first time around by Doctor Petrarco. It's hopelessly inefficient. If I'd seen the gentleman first I may well have forgotten everything he'd told me. But a quick look at his notes and it would probably have all come flooding back and I could have knocked it on the head, one way or the other.

There's more of the same a few patients down the list.

'I've come to have my blood pressure checked and to see if I need to change my medication,' I'm told. And doing the latter would be a whole lot easier if I knew a little more about the patient in question.

Talking of Tatt, and being Tired all the Time, a friend said something really strange to me the other day. She said I looked more tired now, working days, than I'd ever done when I was working nights. 'I thought this new life was going to be good for you,' she'd said. So had I.

So why am I so tired? I wonder if it's because day-time surgeries are so different. We've got something to fight in the day that we don't face as much doing house calls at night. In the day we're always up against the darn clock.

In most surgeries we're allocated ten minutes for every patient – though some I gather go as low as just seven minutes. And that includes the time it takes to write up the patient's notes, normally after he or she leaves the room and before the next name is called. Like everyone I'm a master of abbreviations, some of them official, to speed up the process. But it's still a railway track, a rollercoaster ride that doesn't let up from first to last on your list.

And, of course, some patients just make this challenge even harder.

Today I've just seen a man who seems unaccountably worried about a blister on the inside of his index finger that he feels may be septic – that word again – and should have healed by now. His notes show he's a very low attender and after a brief examination I reassure him that all will be well and tell him that, no, he won't need or get any antibiotics out of me.

He gets up, resignedly and I feel I've won a victory against the clock by having him in and out of the room in less than five minutes. Which is when he says it.

'Oh, and while I'm here,' he says.

It's with those six short words that the real reason for many GP visits comes out. And don't get me wrong. I understand. I know that when we've got something we're worried about or embarrassed by we don't really want to face up to it or talk about it. So we find something else, something easier. We make a GP's appointment to discuss that little thing. We kick off by talking about that. We gauge whether our doctor seems sympathetic enough, whether the surgery is private enough, and then, once we've got that little bit of confidence, we blurt out the real reason for our visit.

The problem, though, is that by the time this happens we've normally got well past the half way point of our allocated time. Often we're right at the end of it. And by definition this 'while I'm here' issue is going to be the big one. It will take more than a few simple words to sort out. And there's no time.

So what do I have to say? 'I am so sorry. I understand that's a worry but you will have to make another appointment to talk about that. You can make an appointment at the desk on the way out. I can make sure you get a slot,' I'll say.

'But I'm here now,' you'll probably say.

And the test of nerves will begin. I'll normally try to be cruel to be kind. 'I am so sorry but this does sound like something you need help with, and that's going to take a bit of time. Make another appointment now and ask about this straight away, the moment you get in. It will be dealt with. We can sort it out for you.' And I'm thinking of all the other patients I've still got to see in this session. I'm thinking that we're probably past time already. Maybe horribly so. I know there are likely to be at least half a dozen people sitting reading TV magazines on sticks in the waiting area. So unless it's a clear medical emergency or public health issue that 'one other thing' has to be looked at another time.

While I'm on the subject, there's no nice way to say this, but doctors normally hate people who turn up with a list of issues.

'I don't come very often so I've got a few things,' we're told by patients, who often pull out a list of things on a sheet of paper. I accept that in many other areas of life this seems an efficient and helpful strategy. But not when you've only got between seven and ten minutes – including the time you need to make any referrals and to write up the patient notes – for every patient slot. And not when a broken printer, a lack of prescription paper or low toner means even more precious seconds will be lost. Then, of course, there are the phone calls. The moment you know you're going to have to ring anyone about anything – blood results, a referral, anything at all – then you know you're going to be half an hour behind on your list. If you're not half an hour behind already.

'I'm sorry, but it would be unfair of me to gloss over all of those things in just a couple of minutes,' I might say to someone with a list. 'Do you want to tell me about the one or two that are worrying you the most, then we can make another appointment for the others?' We all try that as GPs. But it's hard. Once people have raised an issue, it's out there. It can't always be brushed away to another day. Yet with no slack in the system you do dread these multiple issues.

One final rant then I'm done. You know what else GPs don't like, funnily enough? Patients who turn up and tell us how late we're running. When a patient's first words are: 'My appointment was for twenty past nine, you know,' then the rest of the slot is unlikely to go well. We apologise, of course. But some patients don't let it go. 'But it's gone ten o'clock,' they'll point out accusingly and unhelpfully. Sometimes they'll follow up with a burst of: 'And what are you going to do about it?'

To which I'd like to reply that as a doctor I aim to be able to do many things. But turning back time isn't one of them. And the more you moan about the clock the more time goes by.

That said, I know we can't just get irate when we're faced with conversations like this. Sometimes there's a reason behind them that has nothing to do with the time. It's a defence mechanism by our patient. It's a way of smoke-screening the reason they are really here. If there's something they're embarrassed or afraid of raising, then it's so much easier to postpone mentioning it by going on about something else. So, trust me, I am sympathetic and my social antennae do pick up when people complain. But please – tell me what's wrong and let's get on with that.

On a better note, do you want to know some of the patients GPs tend to love? The ones who come for a repeat visit over the contraceptive pill, are a great example. Fast, efficient and easy. I love them. There are far too few of them in any busy day. But when we get them we can make up some valuable lost time. So bring them on. And while it's definitely bad news that otherwise healthy adults clog up surgery waiting rooms with coughs and colds (and to be fair there are less of these than there used to be) they do at least have the benefit of being brief and easy to shift – because all they need is rest and a bit of friendly reassurance.

But back to Tatt – and tired all the time. As I think about it, maybe my friends think I look tired all the time myself because I'm still at the stage where I worry about all this. I feel bad because I cut that patient short too soon, I think. Then it's the opposite. I feel bad because I didn't cut that patient short soon enough. I'm not sure yet how to square this circle and give everyone the service they deserve.

Chapter Fifteen: A Minor Drama.

I'VE signed up for a half day, morning shift in a surgery I've been to several times lately. I like the people there and I know my way around the computers, the rooms and the equipment. I'm relaxed and ready for anything. Just as well, as it turns out.

I spot the guy as I walk through reception and tell the practice manager I'm here. It's an open-surgery session, a walk-in time, so it's when things can get a little more heated.

I do the thing you soon learn to do as a busy GP when you have to walk through the reception area for anything. You can't not look at the people on the chairs. But you don't really want to make any eye contact. As usual, time is precious and you're probably running late already so any impromptu conversations can make a bad job worse. But you can't help being intrigued. You have to want to know what could be ahead of you.

Today I throw one of my vaguest glances around the room as I walk. I see him, in my peripheral vision. The man is huddled up a little on the back row of the chairs. He's probably mid-fifties and is in work clothes with a high visibility jacket and a hard hat stacked on the chair at his side. He's looking ashen grey and distant. It could be the flu, of course. It could be chronic bronchitis or all sorts of other things that are laying him low. Or it could be something a little more serious. I make a mental note of him and wonder whether he's one of mine.

Minutes later I'm unlocking my room door, logging on to the system, getting my kit ready and checking my watch. It's time to go. I click for my first patient. It's a smart businesswoman in her early fifties who says she has never had a dream in her whole life – but has suddenly starting having long, vivid ones from about 4am until she wakes properly at seven.

'It's just the oddest thing,' she says. 'They're a bit about my life, things that are happening. Then they're also about all sorts of other things, just totally unrelated. And they're so true and believable. I feel as if I'm there. What's happening?'

I run through a brief, idiot's guide to what a dream is. 'Your brain is just sorting things out, filing things away. We all dream.'

'But that's the point,' she says. 'I do know what dreams are. Everyone else talks about them. But I have never, ever had one before. I just go to sleep and I wake up. I get on with my day. When other people at work talk about weird dreams sometimes I pitch in and say I don't dream. Everyone thinks it's weird but it's just the way it is. And then, suddenly, about a month ago, it all changed. I was living in this surreal, technicolour fantasy dream world for hours and hours before my alarm went off. I knew I was dreaming. I knew it wasn't real so I'm not afraid of it. They're not nightmares, there's nothing horrible. But I am afraid of why it's happening.'

Suddenly, looking at her strained face, I can tell she is afraid.

'Am I losing my mind? Am I going mad, somehow? Is it mental illness? Early on-set of something? Are the connections in my brain going wrong? It's just the most bizarre, sudden change in me.'

I try to reassure her. 'Our sleep patterns change all the time, for all sorts of reasons. You will have been dreaming, all your life. You're just aware of them now, when you weren't before. But let's just check a few other things to put your mind at rest even more.' I go through the key questions to see if there's anything of concern going on in her life. I give her a quick physical. Her answers, her blood pressure and all her other key signs are totally fine. Her record shows she's a very low attender with no on-going problems. There are no signs of clouds on her horizon.

'And you're not tired? You are sleeping OK, despite the dreams?' I ask.

'That's the odd thing. I'm aware of all these dreams. I pretty much know they begin about four, so I'll only have been in bed four or five hours by then. But I don't feel bad when I get up as usual at seven. Every now and then I have nights when I can't sleep much for one reason or another – and I'm knackered the whole of the next day. But I'm not knackered at the moment. I don't feel as if I'm missing out on any sleep. I'm just worried that there's something wrong in my brain. It's racing away like I'm on LSD or something and that's never happened to me before.'

I smile. I tell my patient everything seems normal. Then I trot out the cop-out. 'Come back if it gets any worse.'

Then I click for my next patient. It's the man from the back row of the waiting room. He's not walking very well. And if anything he looks worse now than he did when I walked past him just a matter of minutes ago.

'I've been working nights,' he begins, a bit of a rasp in his voice. 'I've only just clocked off. I had a bit of a problem.' He

93

puts his hand on his chest as he speaks. 'The lads said to call an ambulance. But I didn't want to go through all of that again. I knew you were opening up here. I was first in line.'

'Tell me about the problem,' I begin.

He describes feeling totally out of breath, feeling sweaty, heavy and suddenly, horribly sick. Oh, and having pain in his chest, as well.

The classic signs of a heart attack, of course start with the crushing pain in the centre chest that radiates down the left arm and up into the jaw. It can includes all the other ancillary symptoms the man has mentioned. But not everyone gets all the big ticket signs. And it sounds crazy, but sometimes people are convinced they're having a heart attack when all they've got is indigestion. Or, of course, something like angina which is far less serious than it sometimes sounds. So I need to know a little more.

'You said you didn't want to go through this again. What's happened before?'

'I had a heart attack at work. About a year ago. Eighteen months.'

As the man speaks sweat starts to break out on his face. A wave of panic spears to hit him and he starts to gulp in his air. So this is serious. The man's not dropping down dead. But I know he's very much at risk. Like I say, a huge number of things could be happening to him. There's what we can call acute coronary syndrome. There's a spectrum of activity and danger in this syndrome. This man is on that spectrum. He needs to be in what we call the cath lab, the catheterization laboratory in the hospital where cardiologists work. They need to find out exactly what is happening. If you have a heart attack time is very much of the essence. One of the very many things that can be going on is that the blood supply to your heart muscle is blocked. And without blood supply that muscle can die – within twenty minutes to half an hour.

I call an ambulance. We need to blue light this man to the hospital so any blockage can be found and removed to save that muscle.

'Everything is going to be fine,' I tell him, one of the very many medical half-lies we tell because at this stage we can never know. 'The ambulance is on its way so we're going to get you to hospital to be checked out. You did the right thing by coming here. And there's other stuff I'll do now.'

As a locum I carry my own bag of kit and drugs around with me most days. I got used to having that at my side when I was working nights all across town and you never knew what you might need or when. I'm sure I shouldn't say it, but some days I leave the bag locked up safely in my car. Thankfully I didn't do so today. The kit I need will be in the surgery somewhere. But it's the first morning of my first day here so I don't want to waste time looking. I get in my bag and start off with that one oh so simple wonder drug. The aspirin. 'Just crunch on that,' I tell him. He's clearly been here before so he does as he's asked with remarkable calmness. Aspirin does very many things, including easing things along and stopping platelets in the blood getting stuck where they have no business to be. And the great thing about giving someone like this an aspirin is that it's a no lose activity. If he is having a heart attack then it will help. If he's not, then it doesn't really matter.

'OK, you've had a GTN spray before, I imagine?' The man nods as I get the spray out of my bag. It's small, a bit like a canister of breath freshener. I fire a burst under his tongue, from where it can get into his blood stream fast. The GTN spray is another 'belt and braces' activity. If he's 'just' having an angina attack then it should be just what he needs. If he's in fact having a full service heart attack then the GTN won't help, but it won't harm either. And what is in the spray? I love telling people this. It's nitro-glycerine, of all things. They discovered it way back in the Second World War when someone spotted that the workers making explosive in the bomb factories weren't getting heart attacks. Researchers took a closer look. They saw that breathing in the nitro-glycerine by-products was affording them some useful protection. Ever since we've realised that an offshoot of this most unlikely of products can save as many lives as it takes.

It's a classic example of how scientists can sometimes stumble upon cures and treatments when they are focusing on something else altogether. It's also a classic example of how useful it is to look at large amounts of medical data. I've not kept up to date with the latest political and civil liberties arguments over a national health data base. Last time I looked all sorts of people were getting angry and saying they didn't want their medical records to be put in some big computer. But you know what? That could save so many lives. Number crunching spots things. It sees patterns and trends. It explores the reasons behind them. And it makes sure that if my builder friend today is having an angina attack then he's almost certainly going to get through it.

And talking of which – where exactly is the ambulance?

'Just give me one moment,' I say, heading out to reception. The staff there are as concerned as me. And one of them has a theory. 'They'll be at the old surgery,' she declares.

That's news to me. 'What old surgery?'

'We just moved. Same street but the numbers don't follow a pattern. The old place is way round the corner to the left. You can't see it from here. They'll be outside there.'

I look at my receptionist friend. Lovely lady but the size of a small car. She's not going to run any marathons soon. So I get the directions, get a different GP in the room with my patient and leg it down the street. She was right. I can see those day-glo colours of the ambulance far, far away and I sprint towards it, waving my arms like a madman.

They still think I'm mad when they've turned around, got to the right address and started to treat my patient.

'It's his heart,' I hear myself say as the paramedics pile in with an oxygen mask and attach him to the portable ECG machine that will give all the clues they need to show what's really going on. I get a quizzical look from the medic closest to me as I speak. 'No shit, Sherlock,' his eyes seem to be saying. 'I'm stating the obvious, sorry,' I say, bashfully. 'I'm still out of breath from the run. But it is his heart.'

And it is indeed. So, with all the right kit at his side the para's get the man off the chair in my surgery and on to one of theirs. They wheel him off, get him in the back of the ambulance and get him on his way.

The rest of us carry on as normal. We're desperately trying to catch up with the list, that is now wildly behind time. But that doesn't matter, of course. Little mini-dramas like this one certainly break up the doctor's day. They put things in perspective as well. It's a lot easier to over-run your slots if you've done a bit of mild, emergency medicine for a change.

And so the rest of this otherwise ordinary day rolls along. It's another big mental health morning. I see patient after patient who is depressed, distressed, confused or otherwise falling through the cracks of their life. Sadly, of course, these are the patients whose appointments are most likely to over-run. They're here to talk, sometimes willingly and at great length, sometimes falteringly, slowly and with great difficulty. Either way, their slots almost always over-run and no amount of time we give can quite be enough.

Did we do well today as a surgery and as a service? We tried, as we always do. But there's always the suspicion that we could have done more. Some GPs are able to walk away from this without much of a backwards glance. Others may well worry about it too much, arguably feeling too guilty and too concerned about the thing we didn't have time to say or do. I try to find a half way point. And as I leave the surgery I tell the cheery staff that I hope I'll be back. Then I head home to shower and wash the stress away. As I do, I realise I'm exactly three months into what I'd mentally allocated as a six month stint of day shifts. I've not met the woman of my dreams. So I'm as far as ever from settling down and starting a family like so many of my peers. If I'm honest I've struggled a bit after so long working at night. I've felt a bit conventional. I've felt like a face in the crowd, just another worker in the herd of life. This isn't as exciting, as varied or as emotional as doing all those 3am house calls. But I'll stick it for another three months. Then maybe I'll do something else altogether.

That's the beauty of being a locum doctor. We always have options. The other day I had a great chat with a fellow GP who does shifts in a prison and a police station. Another of my pals, Ben MacFarlane, has written a book about his time as a ship's doctor, seeing the world from the portholes of the medical centre on a giant cruise ship. Both of them have stories that make my eyes water. So maybe I'll follow their footsteps for a while when my six months are up. I day dream about these possible challenges as I sort out some chores at home. And as I do so I realise I'm smiling to myself. You could say that's mad. But I feel good. And all of a sudden I think back to at least three of the sad patients I'd seen that morning. They felt they were out of options. At any given moment they focused almost entirely on the floor beneath their feet. I wish I'd told them to look ahead. To pick just one thing they'd like to be, see, do or have in six months' time. Did that need to be a realistic goal? Probably not. But looking forward to tomorrow can be the best cure for so many of the issues of today. Yes, it's a bit trite. No, it can't help everyone. But I swear that optimism is one of the best prescriptions I'll ever write.

www.ingramcontent.com/pod-product-compliance
Lightning Source LLC
Chambersburg PA
CBHW031628040426
42452CB00007B/734